dresses

a-line — slip — strapless — empire — shift — cocktail — sheath

backless — jumper — slip — halter — pouf — one shoulder — apron

tent — spaghetti strap ruffle — shirt — wrap — qi pao — maxi — ball gown

dress, drape/points of tension

dress, step by step

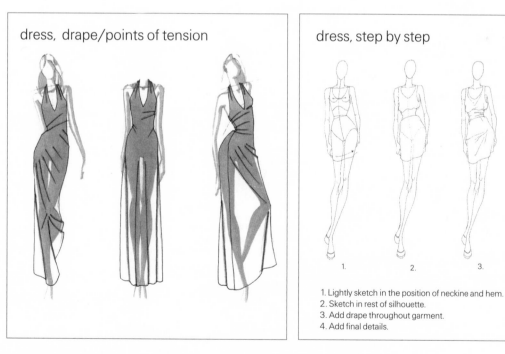

1. 2. 3. 4.

1. Lightly sketch in the position of neckine and hem.
2. Sketch in rest of silhouette.
3. Add drape throughout garment.
4. Add final details.

zippers

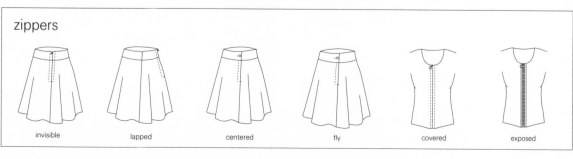

invisible — lapped — centered — fly — covered — exposed

jackets

bolero	hiking/windbreaker	jean	blouson	biker	baseball	hoodie
anorak	quilted	cardigan	chanel	nehru	6 button d-b blazer	s-b blazer
4 button d-b blazer	pea coat	duffle	safari	parka	shearling	belted
wrap	poncho	swing	babydoll	designer pleated	overcoat	trench

barrel   cape

jacket, step by step

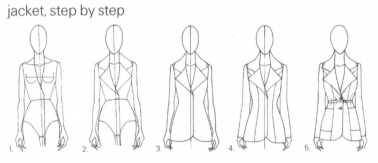

1. Draw upper croquis + c-f line. Decide shape of neckline, mark position of lapel overlap and top button.
2. Begin drawing collar from back of neck.
3. Draw in hem and silhouette of sides from the armholes. The jacket is fitted at the waist.
4. Draw in sleeves from shoulder to waist. They appear more natural with a slight bend.
5. Draw in the buttons on the c-f line with horizontal b/holes. Draw in belt, pocks from p-lines to s-seams.

jacket, constructional details

- collar roll
- sleeve cap
- set-in armhole
- inverted pleat in lining
- princess seam
- two piece sleeve
- princess seam
- welt pocket
- vent
- decorative buttons

jacket, drape/points of tension

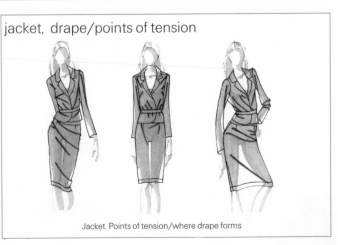

Jacket. Points of tension/where drape forms

sleeves/armholes

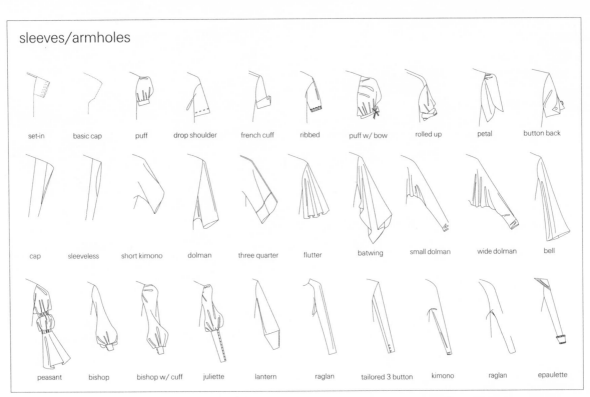

set-in	basic cap	puff	drop shoulder	french cuff	ribbed	puff w/ bow	rolled up	petal	button back
cap	sleeveless	short kimono	dolman	three quarter	flutter	batwing	small dolman	wide dolman	bell
peasant	bishop	bishop w/ cuff	juliette	lantern	raglan	tailored 3 button	kimono	raglan	epaulette

collars

knitted turtle	crush	mandarin	stand up	peter pan	pointed	stand up	button down	bertha	pilgrim
overlap fichu wrap	cowl	cross muffler	sailor	stock tie	scarf through	high stand	sculptured	ribbed
funnel	ruffle	trench	biker snap	notched	cascade	fish mouth	hood front	hood side

lapels

notched	semi-notched	cloverleaf	saddle-stitched	L-shaped
peaked	ulster	tab	framed	
fish mouth	shawl	chanel	frill	

darts

armhole	radiating	french
bust waist	inverted Y	shoulder waist
shoulder	T	

shirts/tops

camisole · bustier · vest/waistcoat · sleeveless · blouse · polo

henley · single placket shirt · tailored one pocket · pin tuck · western shirt · tuxedo

ruffle front · military · turtleneck · sailor · wrap around · bodysuit/leotard

sweatshirt · sweater · peplum · smock · tunic · gypsy

necklines

round · v · u · oval

square · boat · diamond · funnel

round keyhole · funnel · bound keyhole · off/shoulder

off/shoulder · halter/cowl · cowl · asymmetrical

halter · halter · crew

henley · gathered · bottleneck

top, step by step

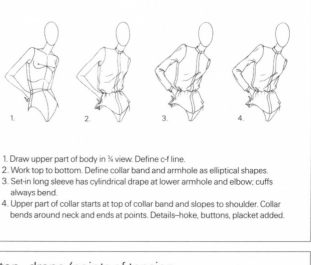

1.   2.   3.   4.

1. Draw upper part of body in ¾ view. Define c-f line.
2. Work top to bottom. Define collar band and armhole as elliptical shapes.
3. Set-in long sleeve has cylindrical drape at lower armhole and elbow; cuffs always bend.
4. Upper part of collar starts at top of collar band and slopes to shoulder. Collar bends around neck and ends at points. Details–hoke, buttons, placket added.

top, drape/points of tension

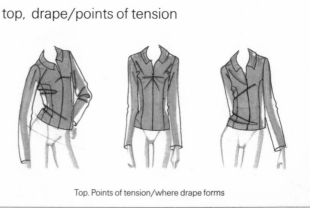

Top. Points of tension/where drape forms

skirts

mini jean style • tiered flounce • crisscross drape • cascade wrap • pleated • godet • gore • culottes • layered

button front slit • knife pleat • half peplum • bias ruffle • dirndl • sarong • cowl • straight • pencil

tulle • full • high low • prairie • trumpet • pleated • handkerchief • wrap

short skirt/long skirt, drape/points of tension

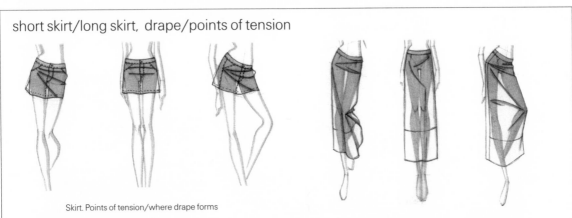

Skirt. Points of tension/where drape forms

pleats and gathers

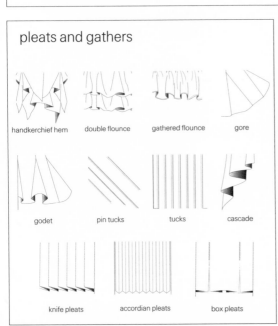

handkerchief hem • double flounce • gathered flounce • gore

godet • pin tucks • tucks • cascade

knife pleats • accordian pleats • box pleats

skirt, step by step

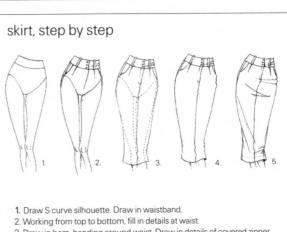

1. Draw S curve silhouette. Draw in waistband.
2. Working from top to bottom, fill in details at waist.
3. Draw in hem, bending around waist. Draw in details of covered zipper.
4. Plot position of main folds–at crotch and from hip to knee. Shade in folds with side of pencil.
5. Draw in other detailing. Shade folds. Note shadows under belt.

pants

hotpants	running shorts	bloomers	shorts	board shorts	overalls	knickers	capri	skinny	straight leg	relaxed

plain front	five-pocket jeans	stove pipe	trousers	bell bottoms	high waist	flare	bush pants	cargo pants	pleated	stirrup

jodhpur	wrap	lounge pant	sweatpants	harem pants	soave	sailor	paper bag	palazzo	wide legged	jump suit

pants, drape/points of tension

Pants. Points of tension/ where drape forms

waistbands

denim belted	gathered paperbag	d ring pleated	vintage high waist wrapover

buckles/belts

turquoise /silver	wood clasp	steel	leather

braided leather	h/shoe metal & leather clasp	iron knot closure

pants, step by step

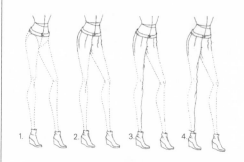

1.   2.   3.   4

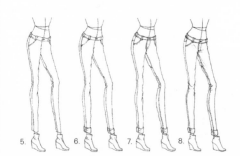

5.   6.   7.   8.

1. Draw in waistband as 2 elliptical lines.
2. Draw in lightly hips and pelvis, c-f & princess lines.
3. Draw in inside of support leg; show folds at knee
4. Draw in hemline of sup leg curving from ankle.
5. Draw in outside edges of legs from waist to ankle.
6. Begin detailing–pockets, loops, cuffs, here for a jean.
7. Add zipper on right–same as men's jeans using line of
   d-needle stitching also seen at waistband and inseam.
8. Add drape at crotch, upper leg and knee

swimwear/lingerie

tankini	two piece	vintage	bikini	one piece	tank top	sarong + top	cover-up
slip	negligee	babydoll	teddy	camisole	bustiere	sports bra	
bra top	cotton bra	full underwire	half underwire	lace bra	girdle	garter	

buttons/buttonholes

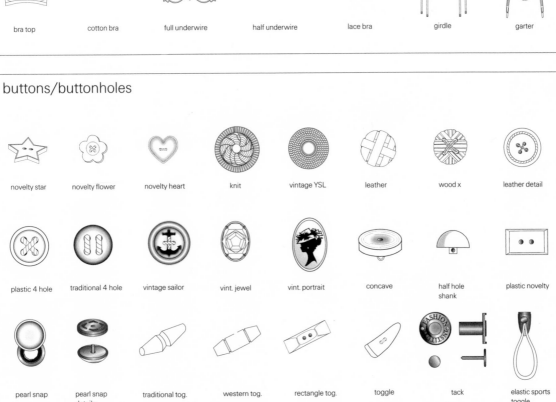
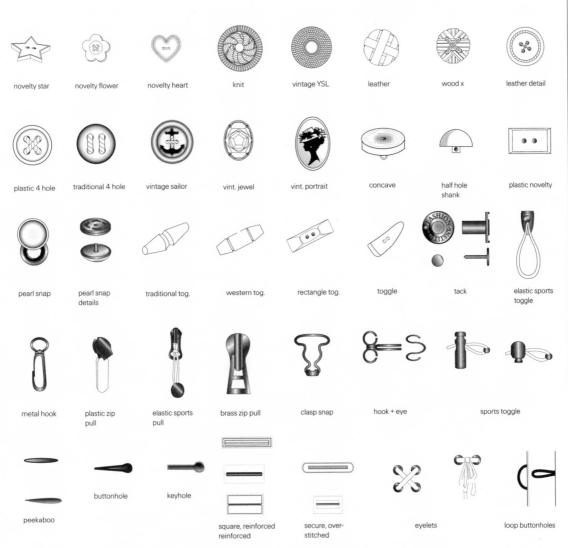
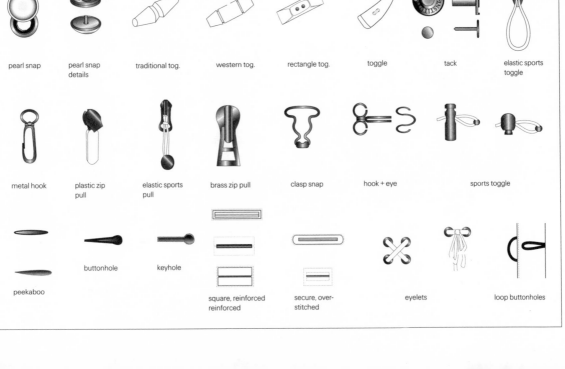

novelty star	novelty flower	novelty heart	knit	vintage YSL	leather	wood x	leather detail
plastic 4 hole	traditional 4 hole	vintage sailor	vint. jewel	vint. portrait	concave	half hole shank	plastic novelty
pearl snap	pearl snap details	traditional tog.	western tog.	rectangle tog.	toggle	tack	elastic sports toggle
metal hook	plastic zip pull	elastic sports pull	brass zip pull	clasp snap	hook + eye		sports toggle
peekaboo	buttonhole	keyhole	square, reinforced reinforced	secure, over-stitched		eyelets	loop buttonholes

pockets

 single welt

 welt

 formal welt

 welt w/ flap

 western welt w/flap

 doghouse bound welt

 patch

 patch

 patch w/flap

 patch w/ flap

 button patch

 rounded patch

 basic cargo

 cargo

 d ring cargo

 ribbed cargo

 sports cargo

sports

 kangaroo

 gathered flap

 inverted button

 coin

 western flap

 tabbed button flap

 stationery

 side bucket

glasses

 half frame

 reading

 oxford

 cat

 rimless

 bevelled

 wellington

 queen

 half rim

 pince-nez

 round

 boston

 jackie o

oval

 vintage

 tear

 aviator

 wrap

 shield

 thick frame

 flexington

 flat top

square

 lolita

trims

 leather braid

 beaded tribal

 gimbal ring

 safety pins

 iron-on

 folded flower ribbon

 venice lace

 beaded venice appliqué

 swarovski motif

 pyramid metal stud

 frog closure

 fringe

 suede fringe

 pearl snap epaulette

 fringed concha

 taffeta bow

feather trim

bullion crest

shoes

kitten	cone	chunky	spoon	stiletto	wedge	pointed	square	almond	peep	keyhole	round

flip flop	finger shoes	teva	sandal	tennis	running	moccassin	deck shoe	penny loafer	

wing tip	saddle	motorcycle boot	ballet	clog	mule	sling back	pump	t-strap	

ankle strap	mary jane	wedge	ankle boot	lace up	snow boot	western boot	over the knee		

hats

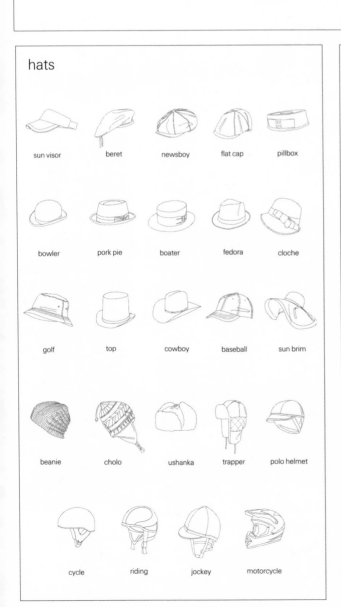

sun visor	beret	newsboy	flat cap	pillbox
bowler	pork pie	boater	fedora	cloche
golf	top	cowboy	baseball	sun brim
beanie	cholo	ushanka	trapper	polo helmet
cycle	riding	jockey	motorcycle	

bags

saddle	clutch	miniaudiere	evening
wristlet	chanel	bowling	shoulder
handbag	hobo	tote	fringe
satchel	messenger	knapsack	barrel

hairstyles

chignon

crown braid/plait

side swept bang

razor cut

asymmetrical

wind swept updo

retro beehive

bob

high volume ponytail

modern beehive

curly

eye, step by step

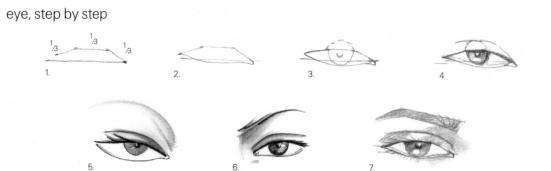

1.

2.

3.

4

5.

6.

7.

1. Draw horizontal line level with inner point of eye. Draw the upper line of the eye with three equal lines sloping at sides and flat on top.

2. The lower line of the eye arcs up from right to left (on left eye, on right eye left to right) to the outer point of the eye.

3. Draw in iris, one third the width of the eye. Two thirds of it is visible, the rest under the eyelid.

4. Upper part of iris slightly darker because of cast shadow from iris. Pupil is darkest point of eye with often a white pinpoint of light.
   Outer edge of iris is also dark.

5–7. Lashes are drawn with curved lines that sweep outwards from the upper and lower edges of the eye. The line at the top of the eyelid where it meets
   the eye socket is parallel to teh upper line of the eye. Eyebrows are wider than the eye, arching up from the eye's edge.

hairstyles

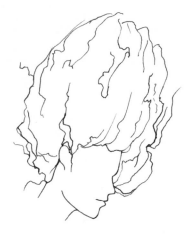

inspired by 18th century

beach waves

lash grazing bangs

bohemian / strong side part

loose curls

romantic / one side up

hand positions

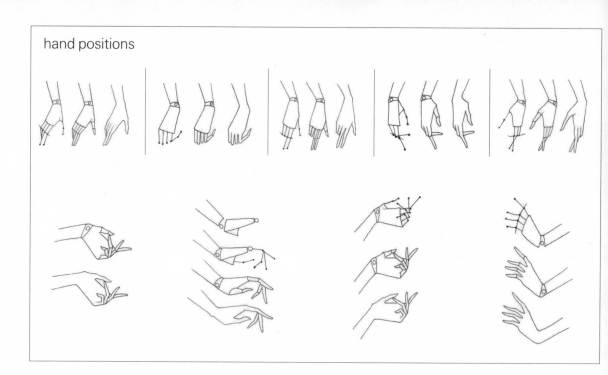

front view face

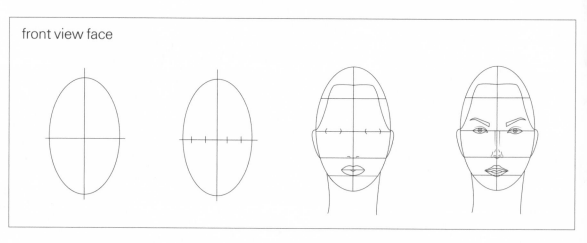

three quarter view face

side view face

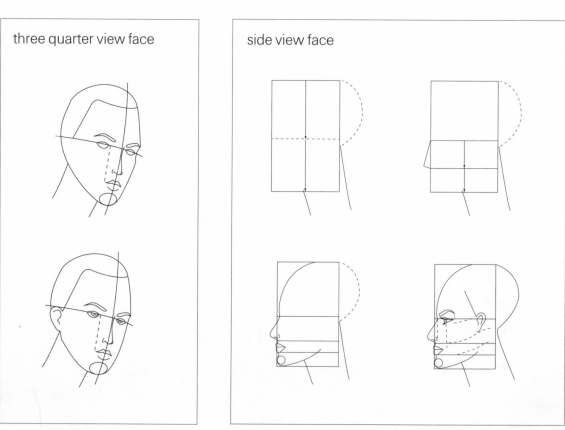

portfolio presentation options

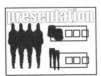   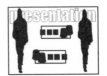

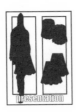  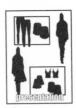

S curve variations

croquis, three-quarter view, side view

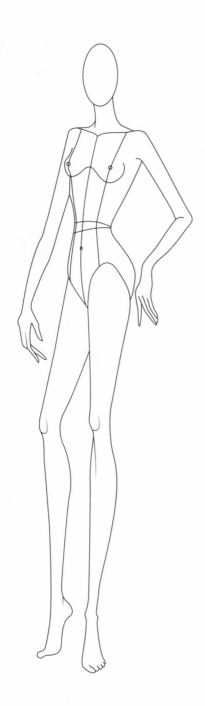

clothes on the figure, jacket/pants

clothes on the figure, blouse/skirt

clothes on the figure, dress

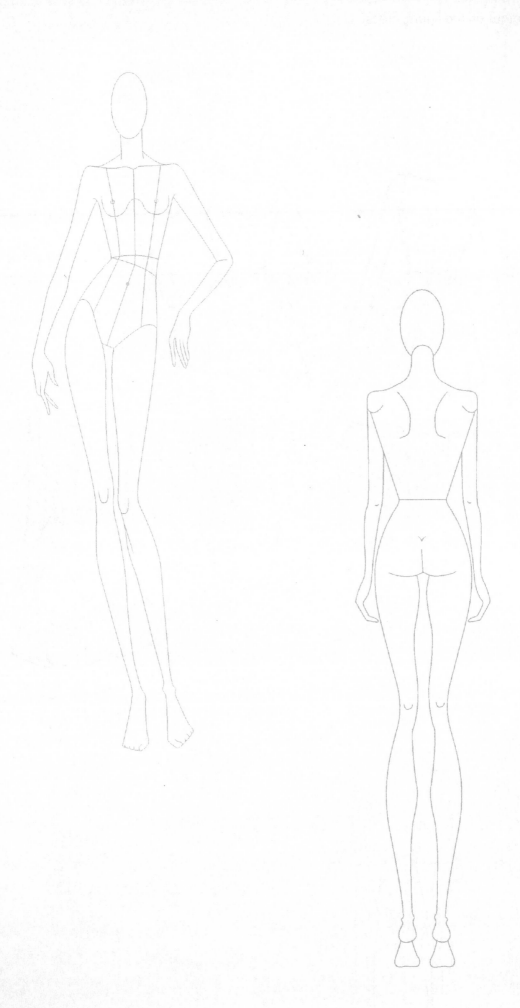

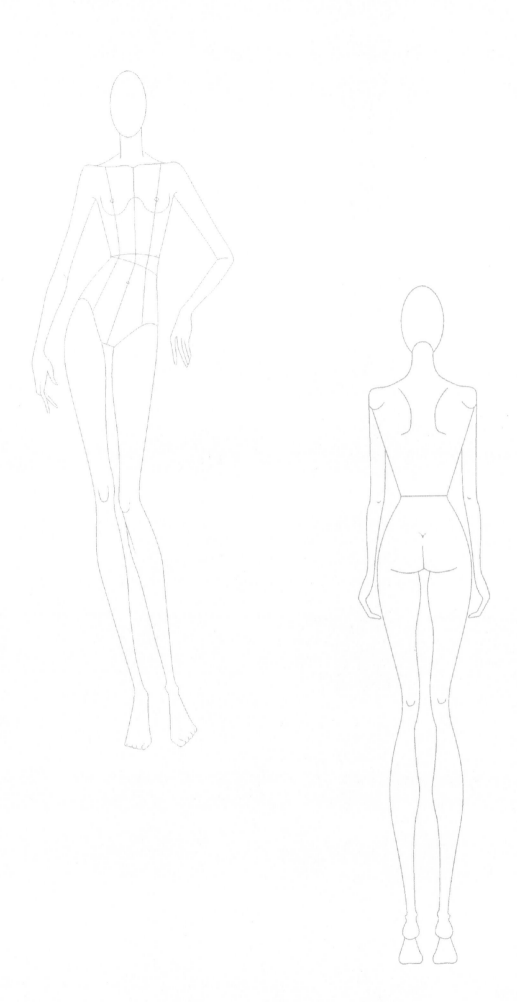

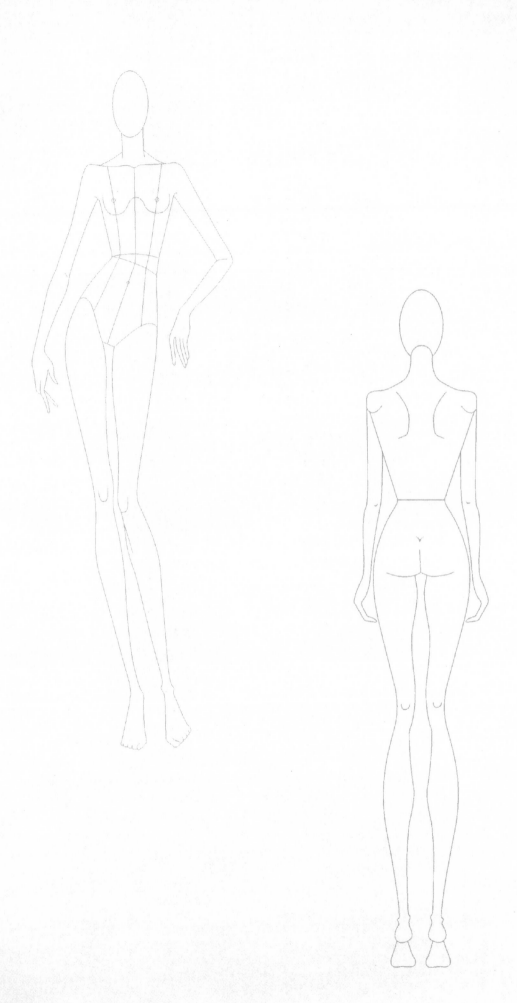

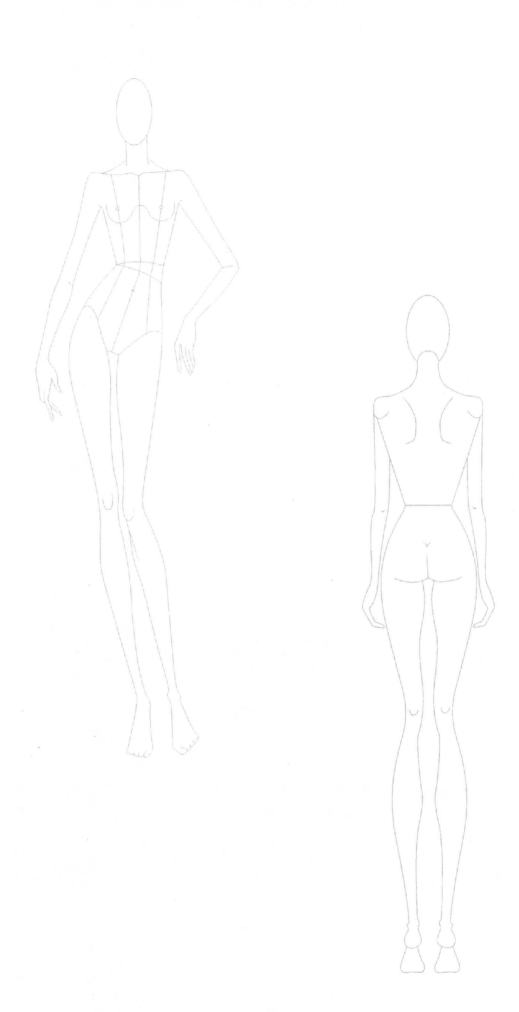

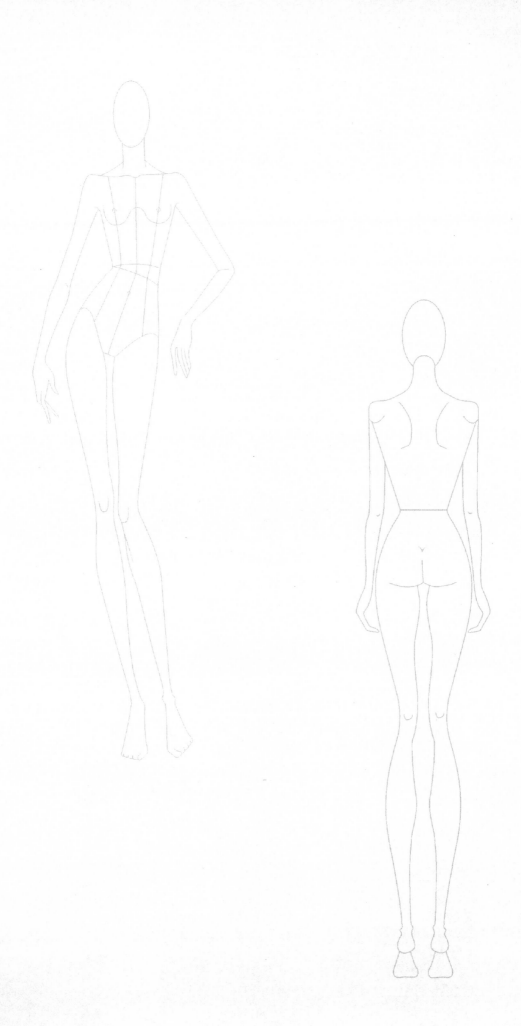

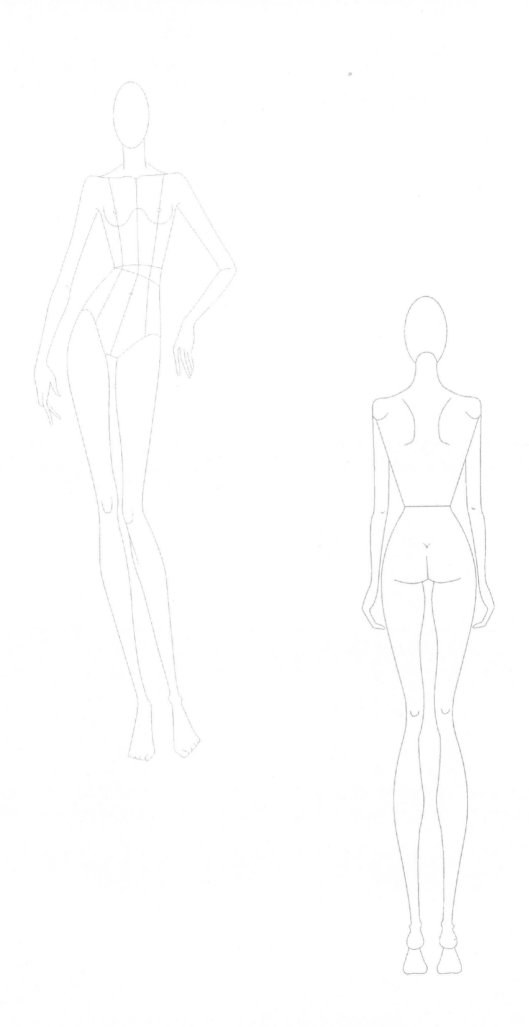

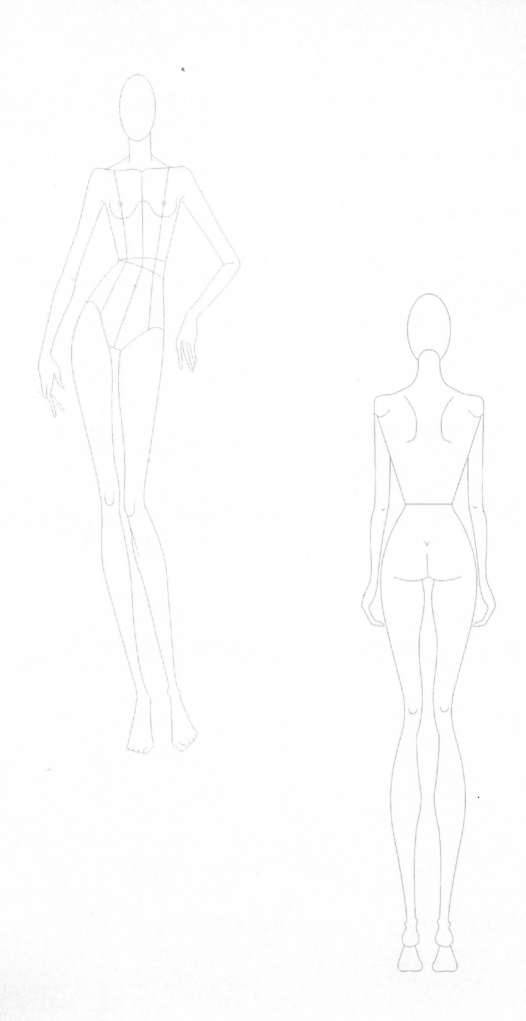

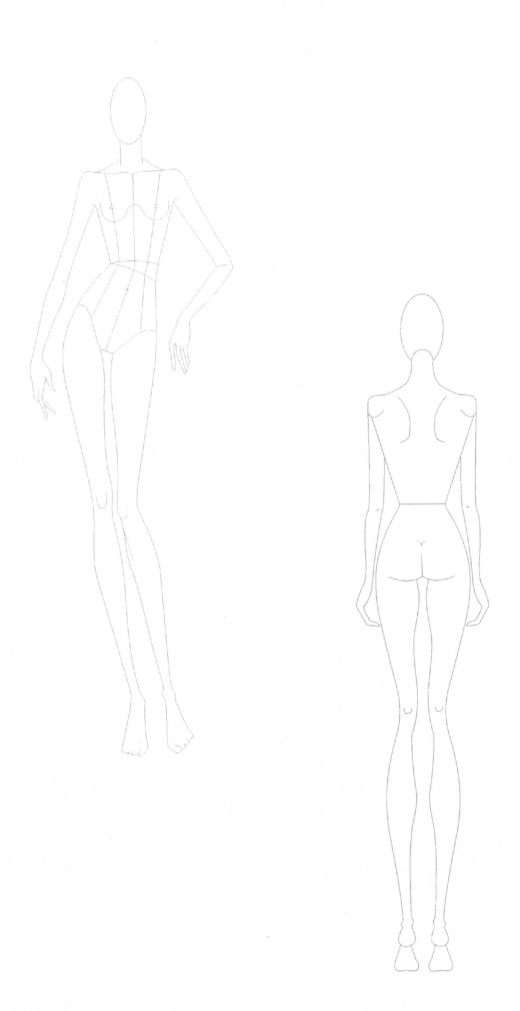

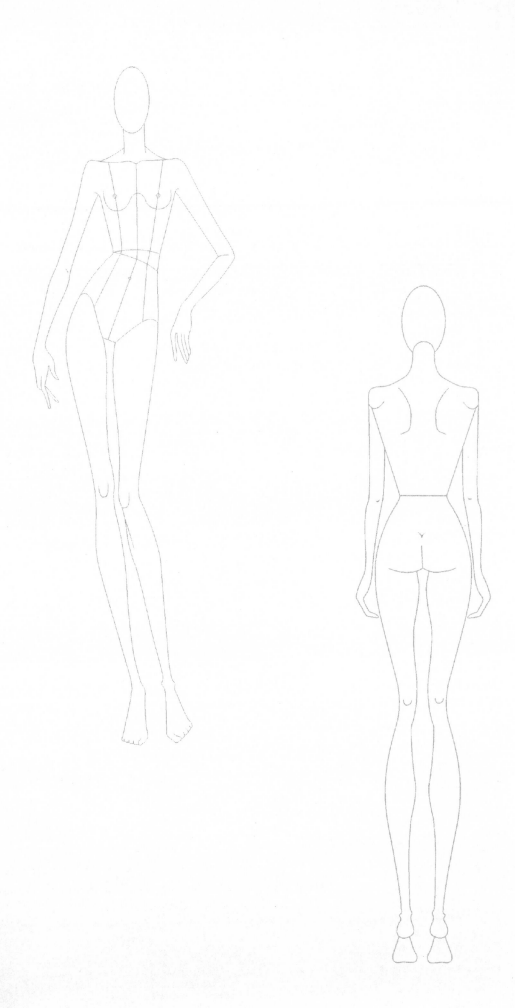

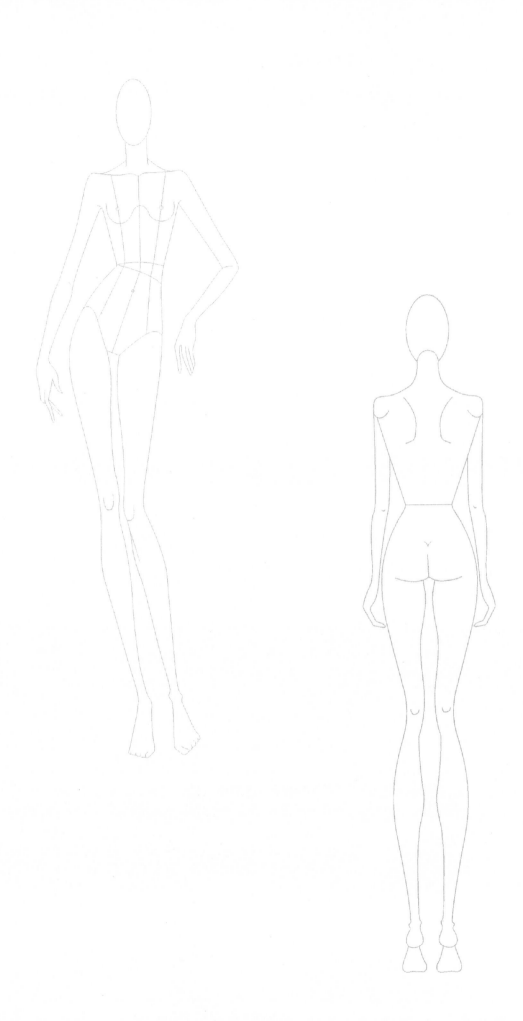

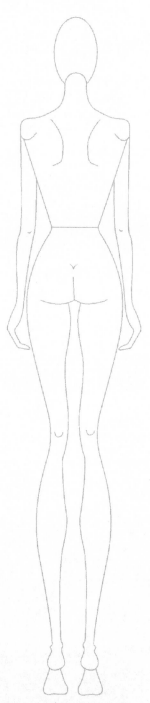

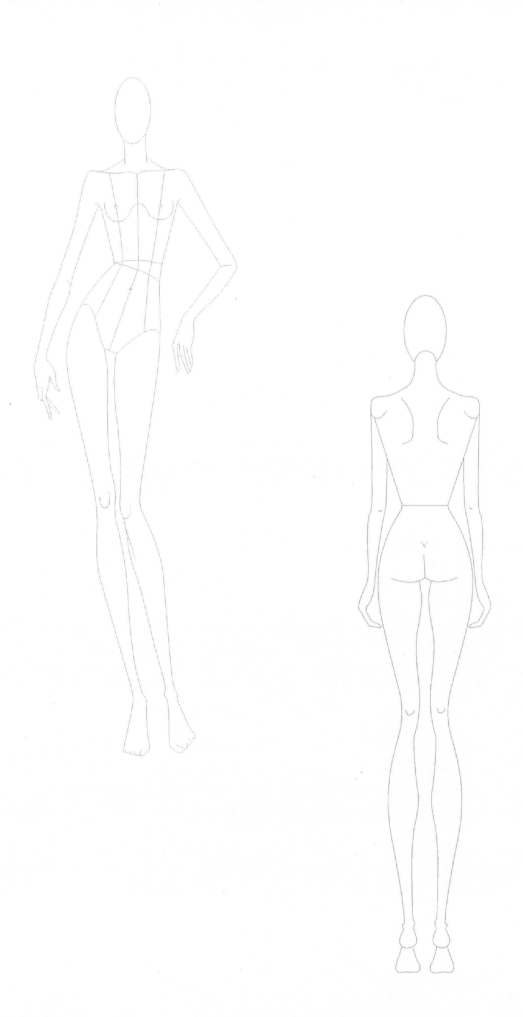

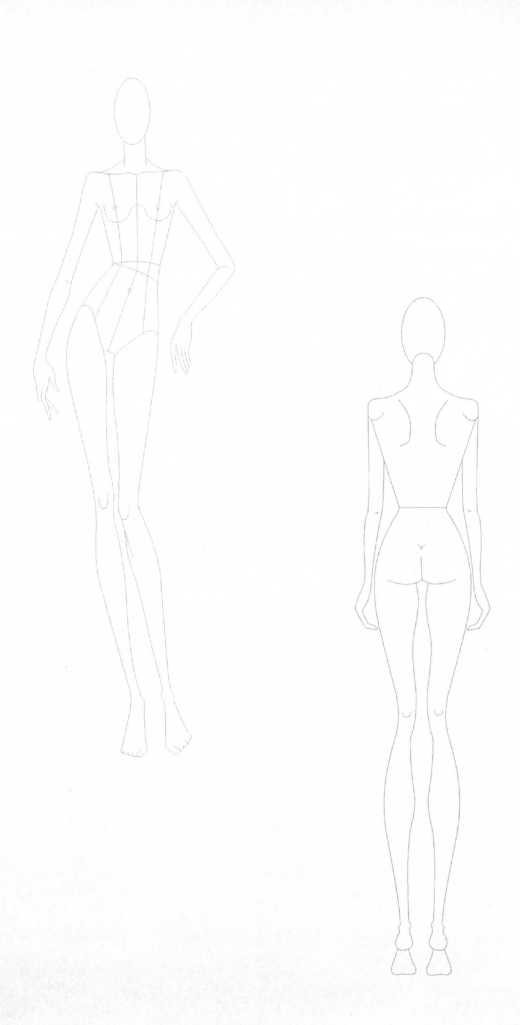

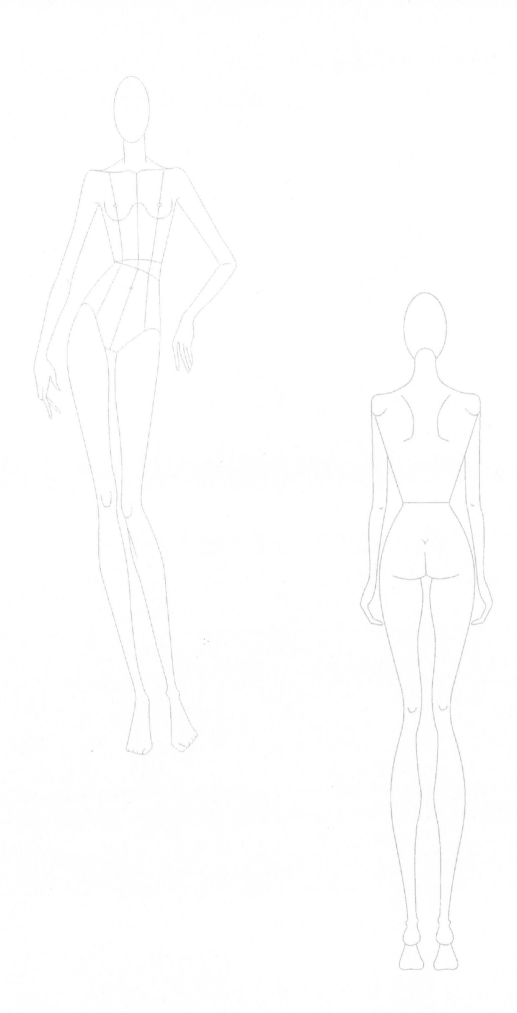

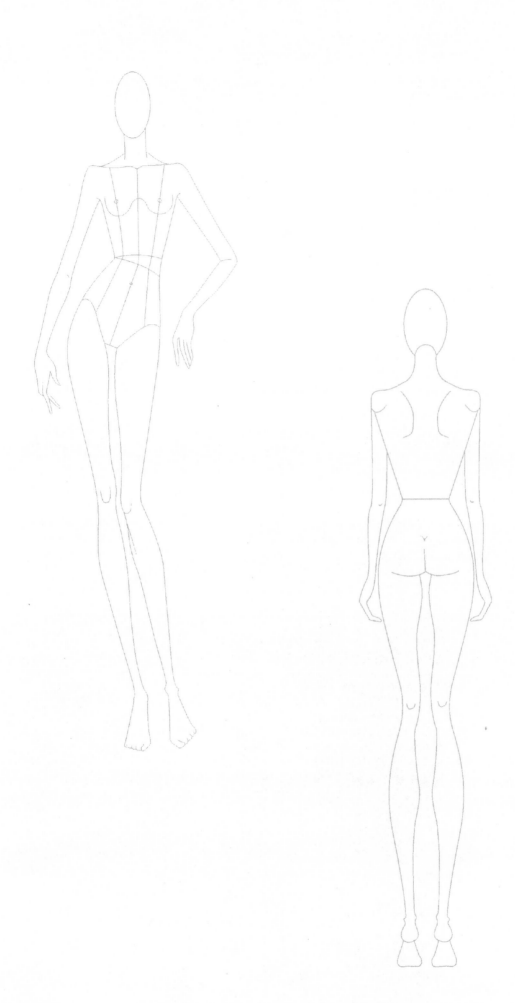

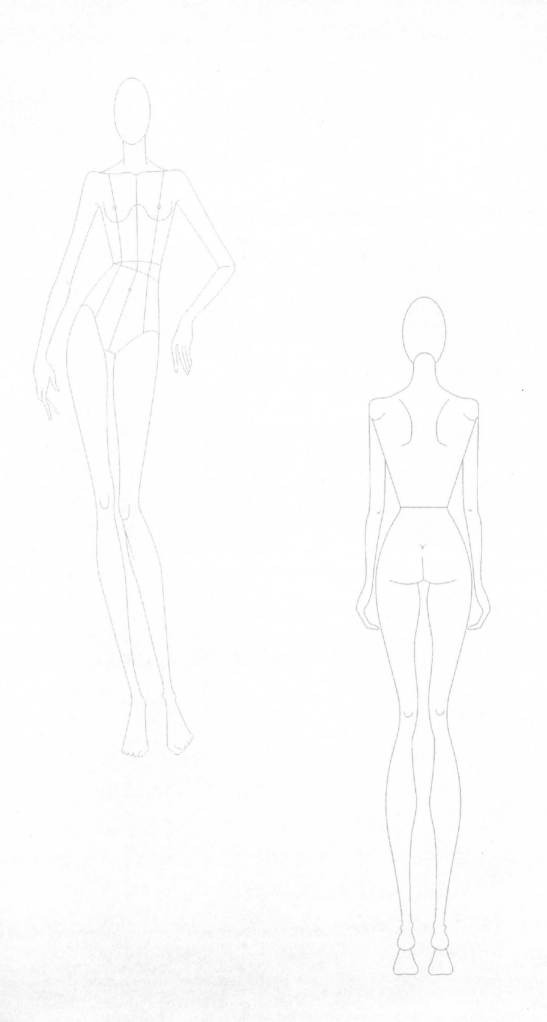

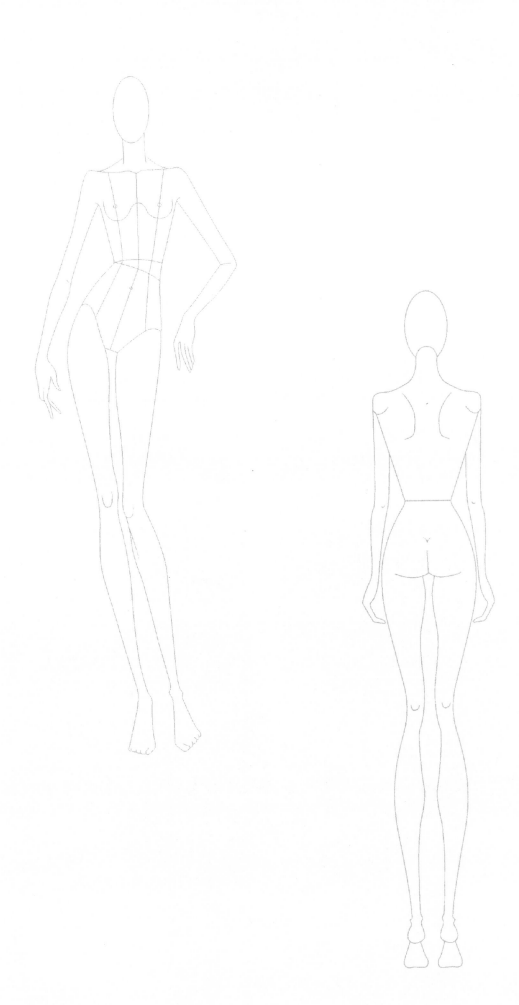

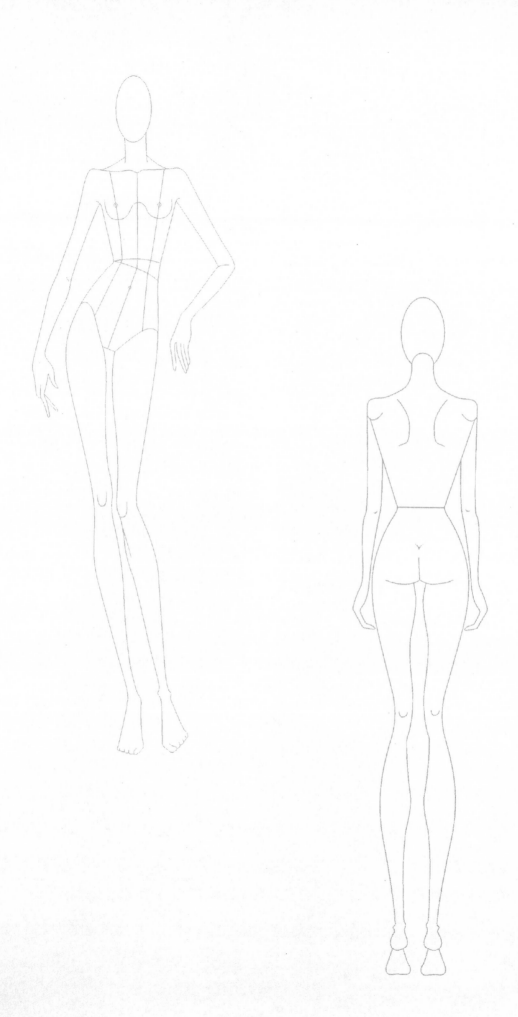

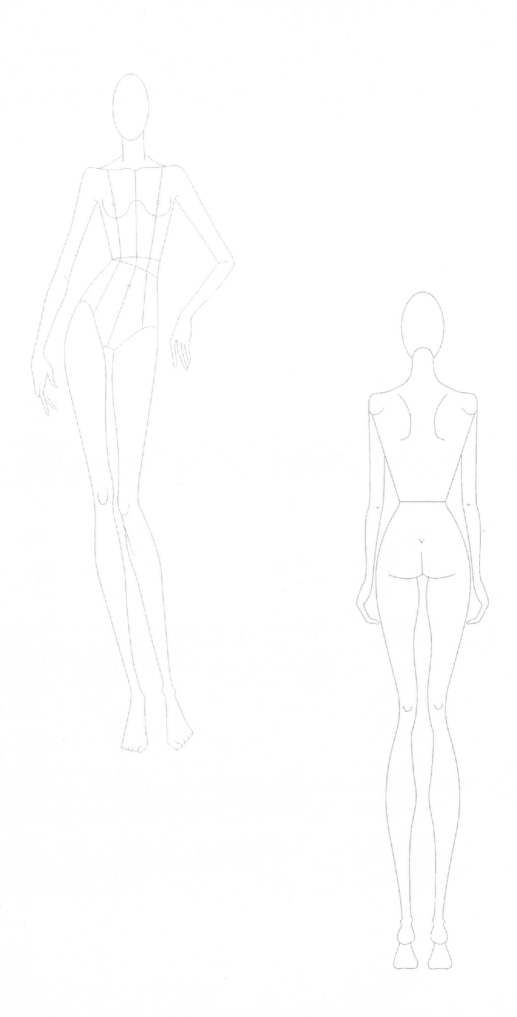

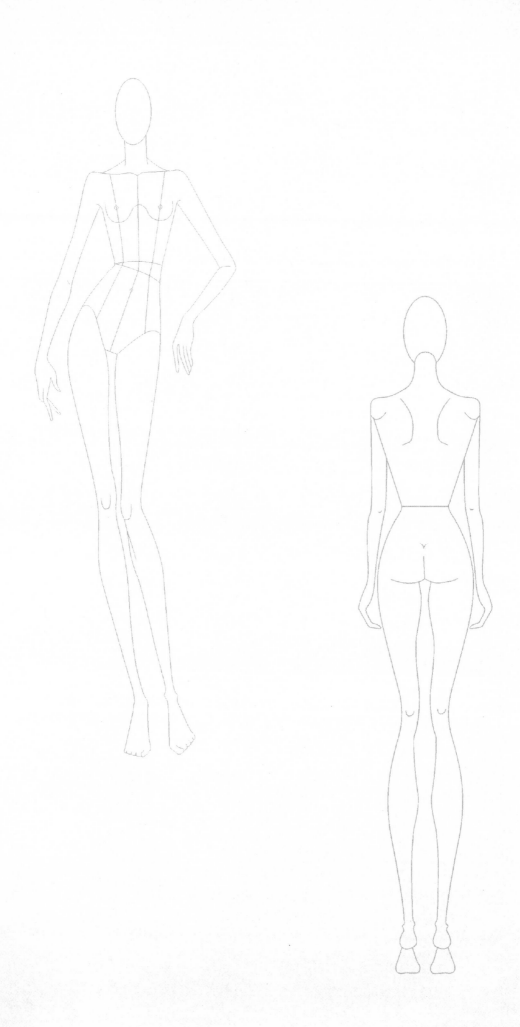

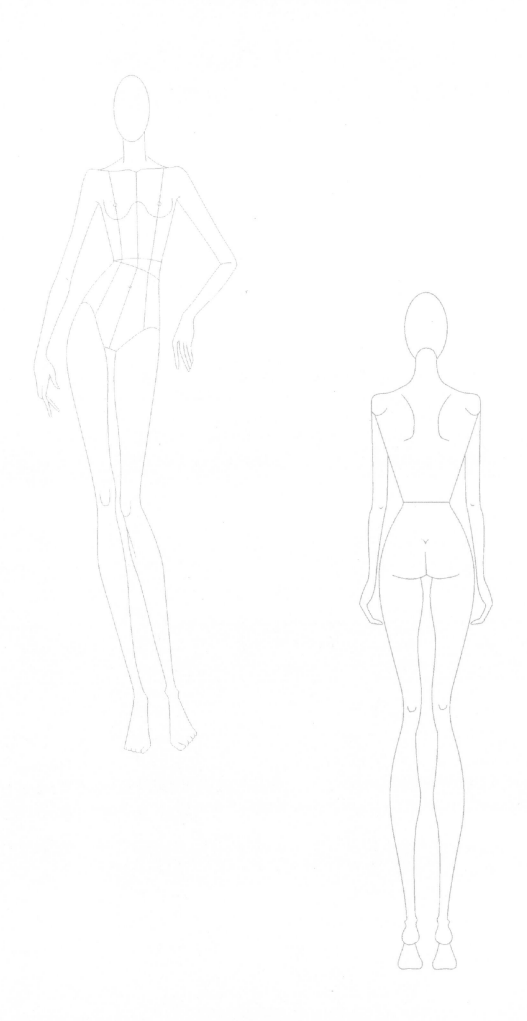

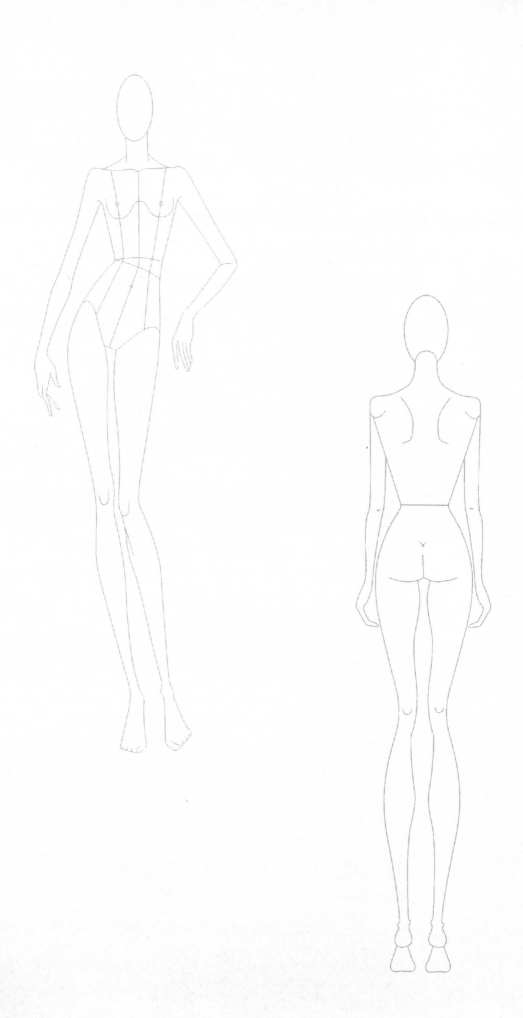

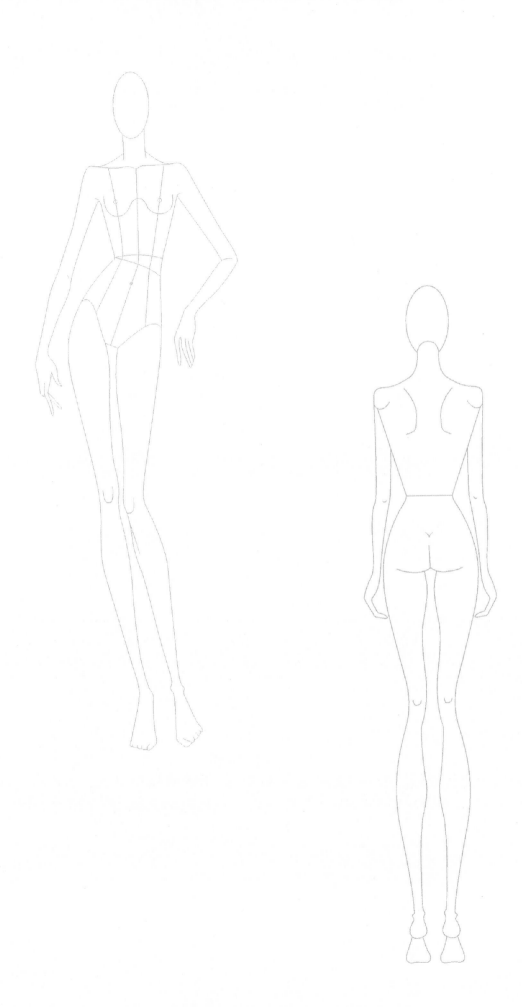

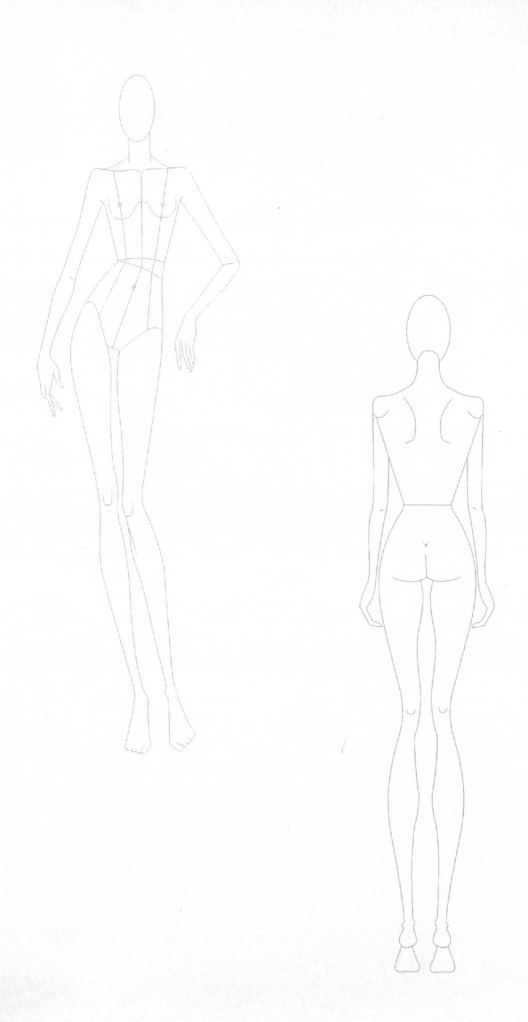

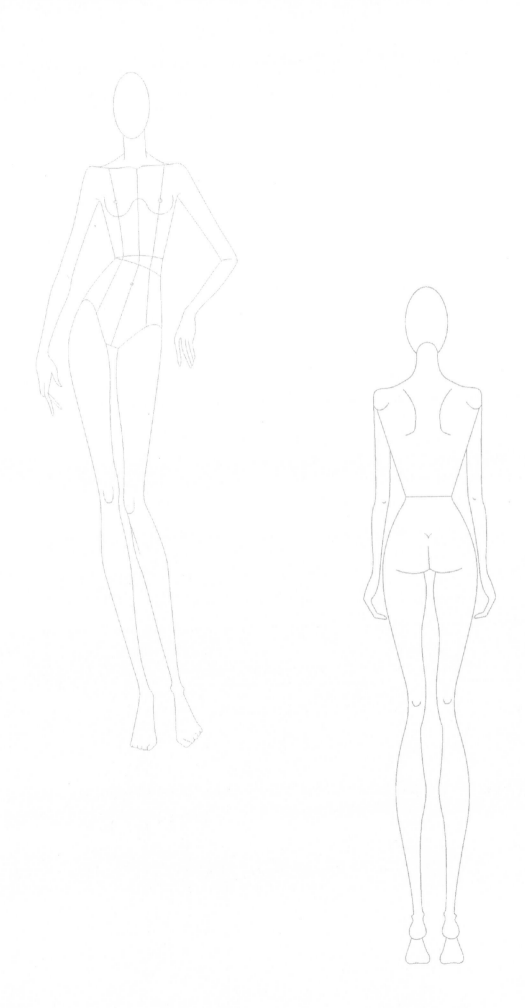

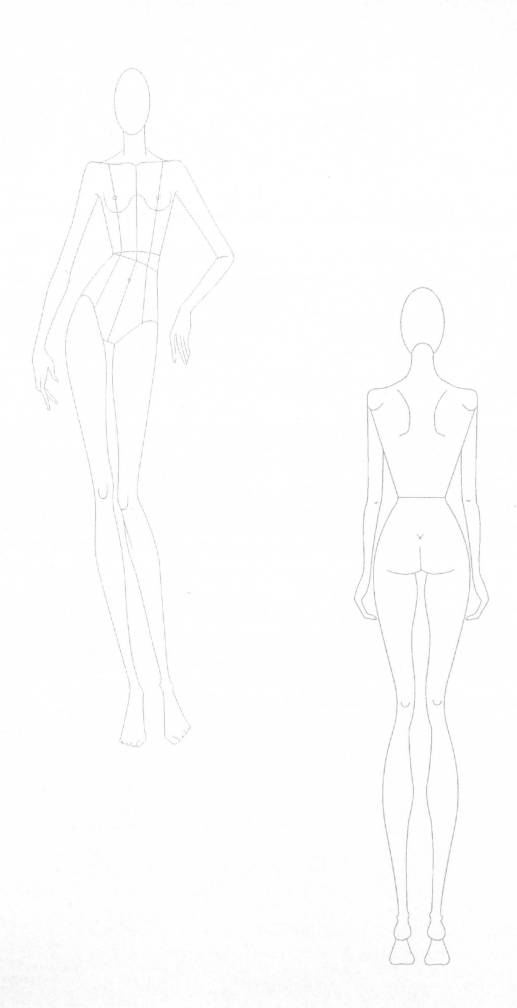

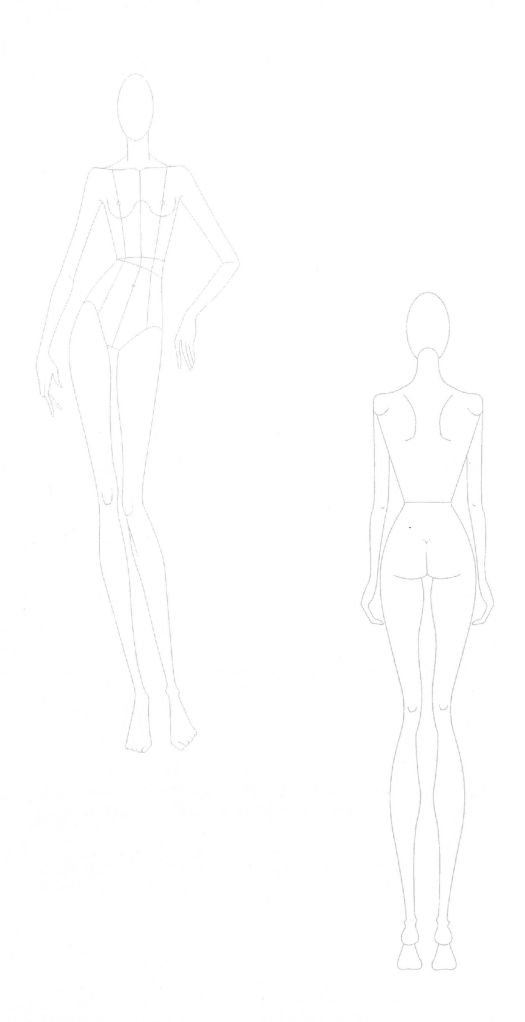

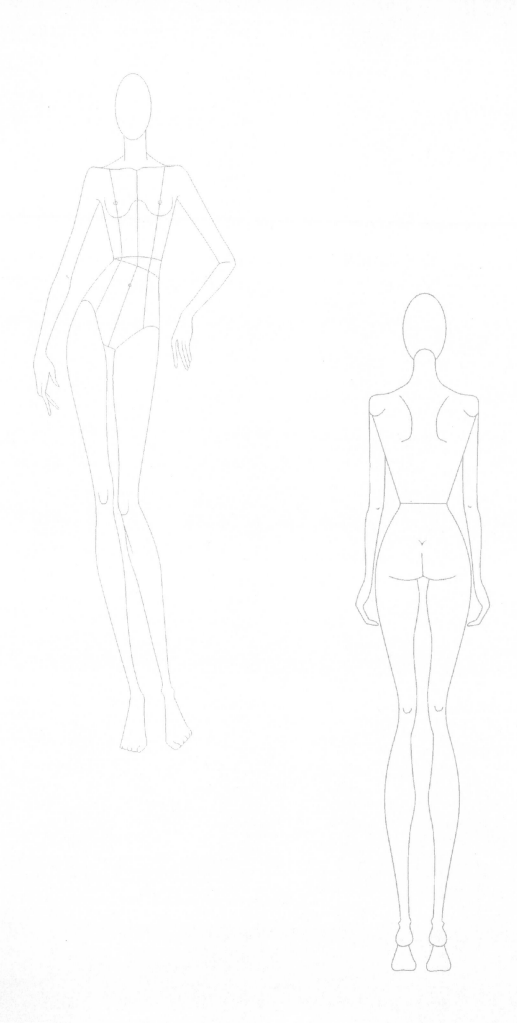

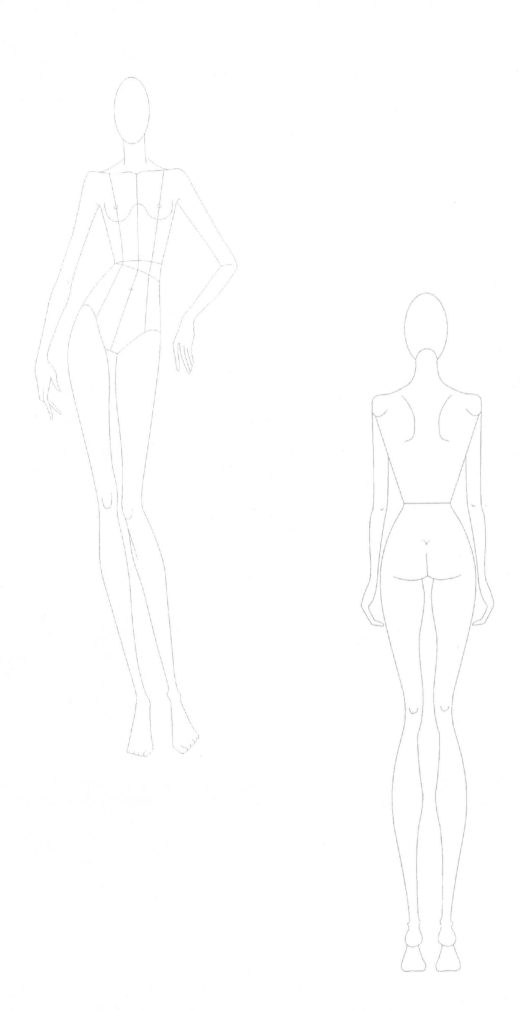

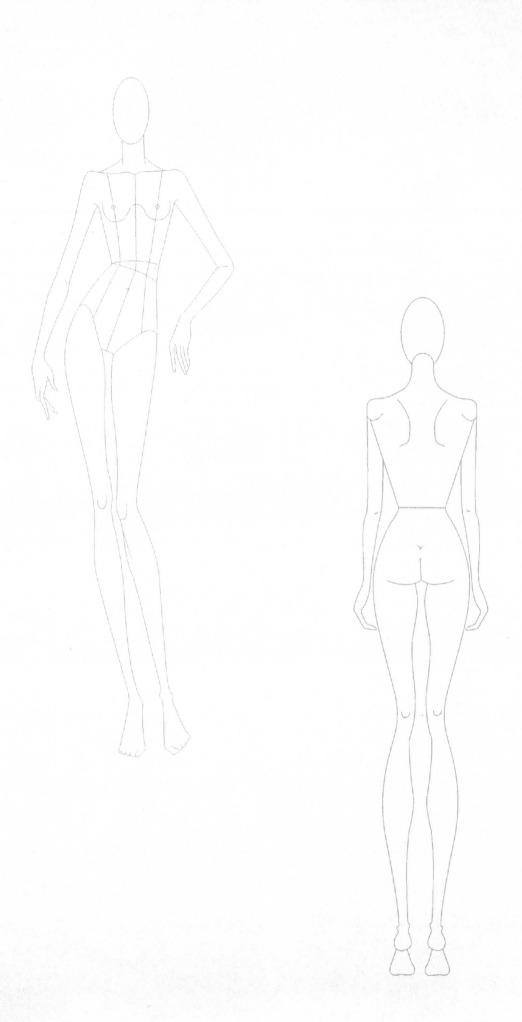

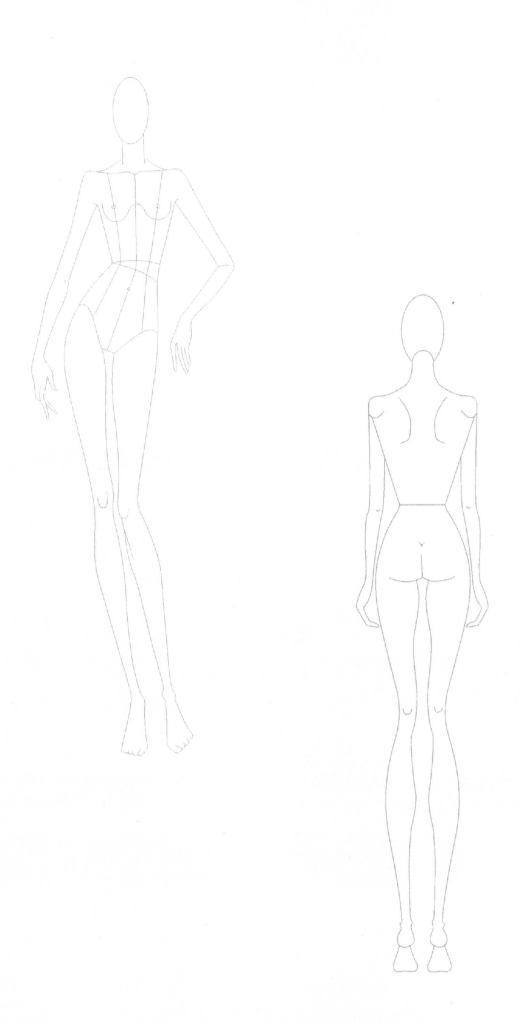

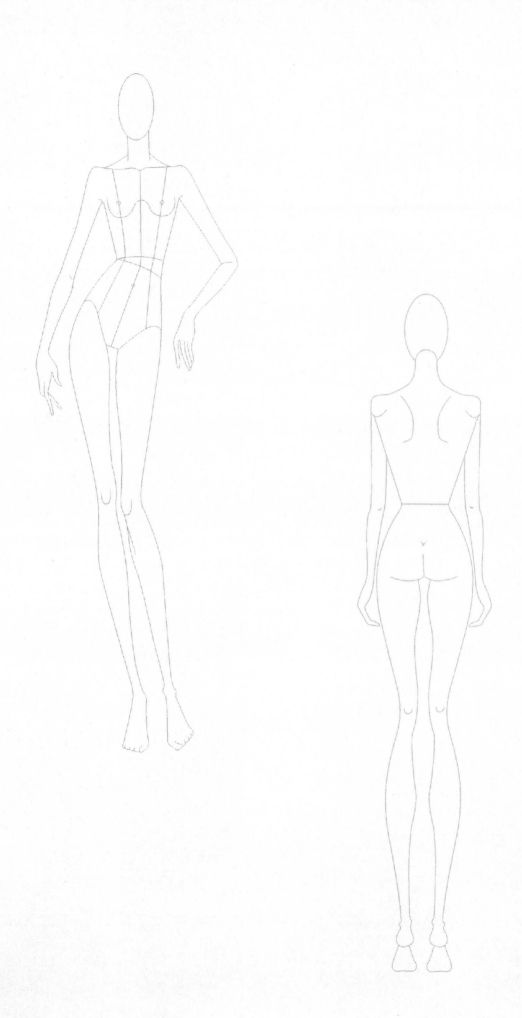

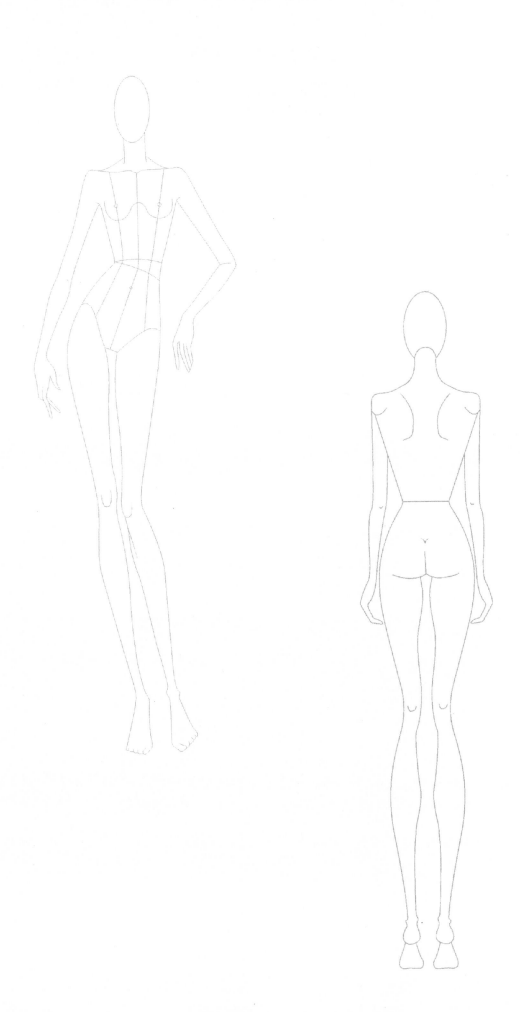

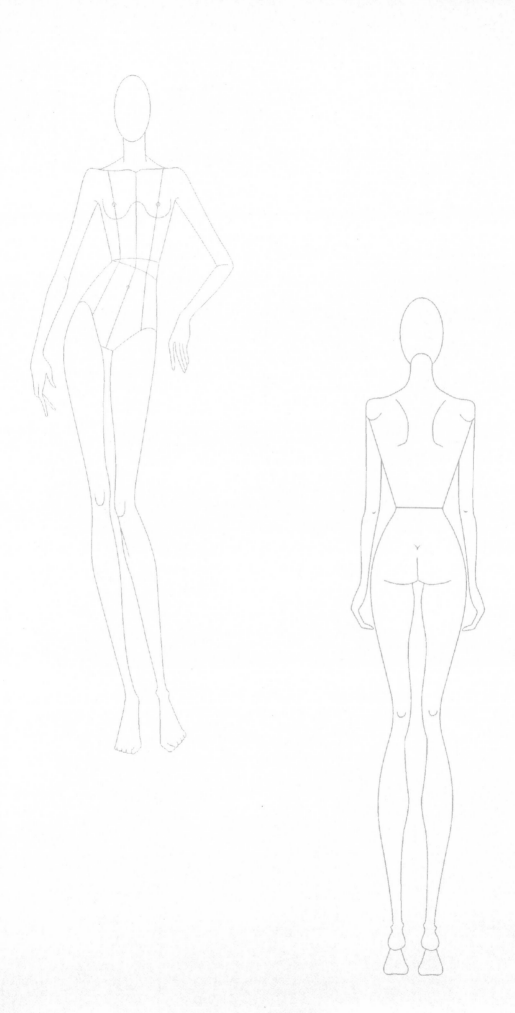

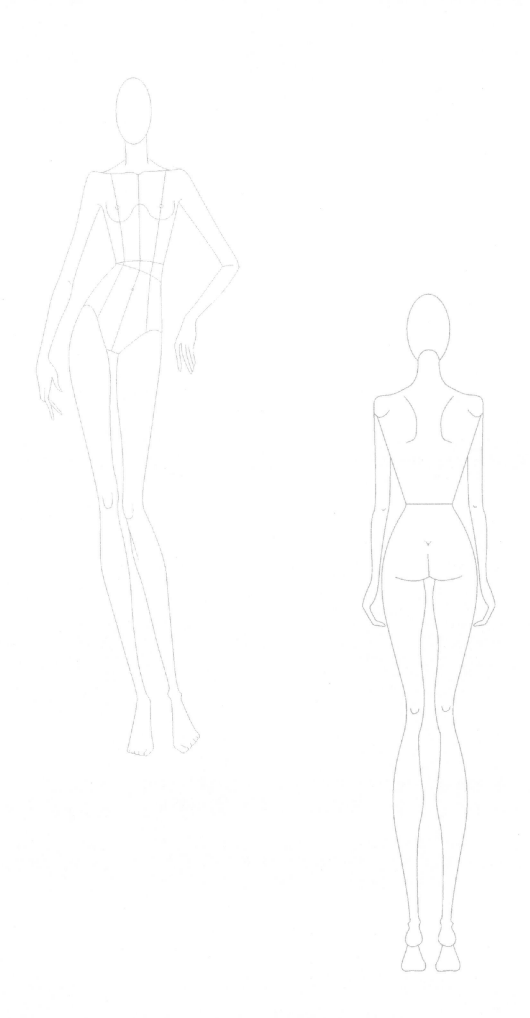

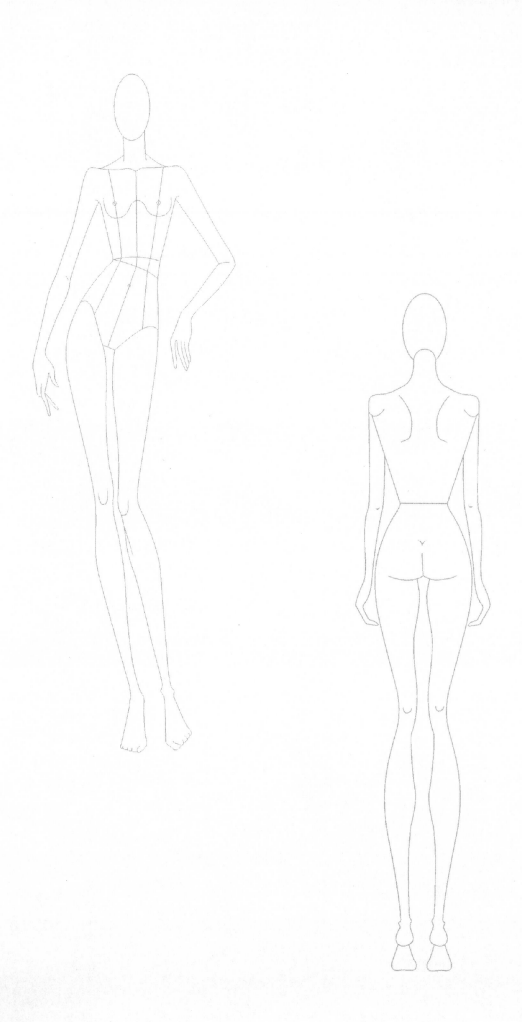

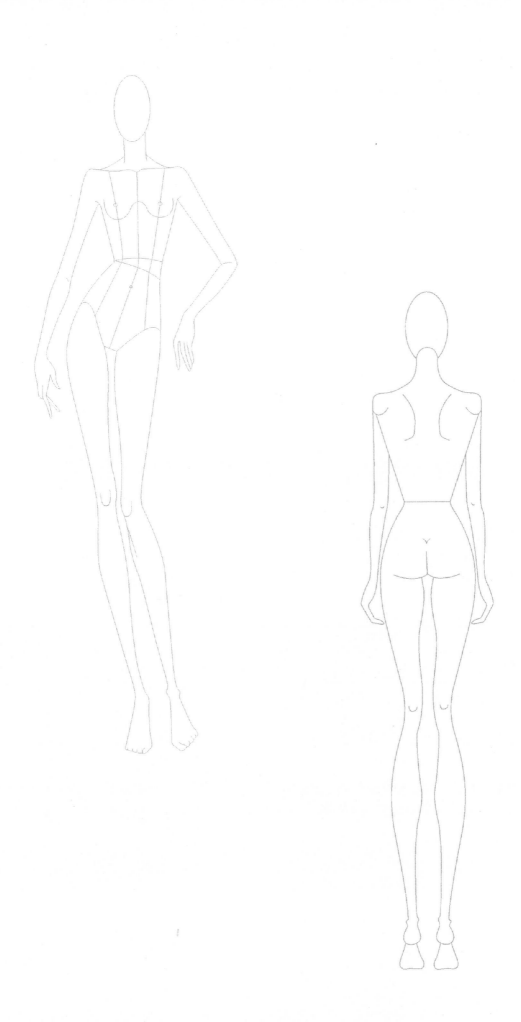

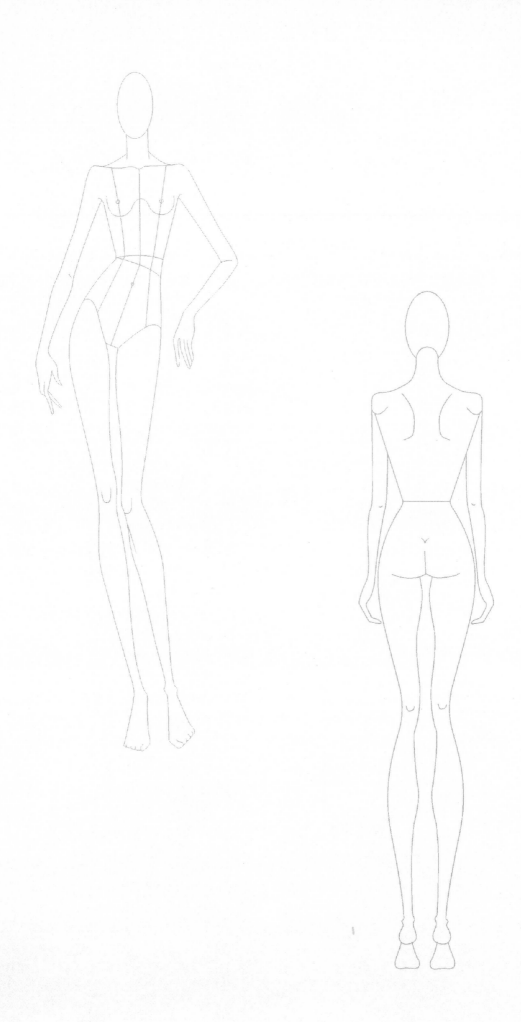

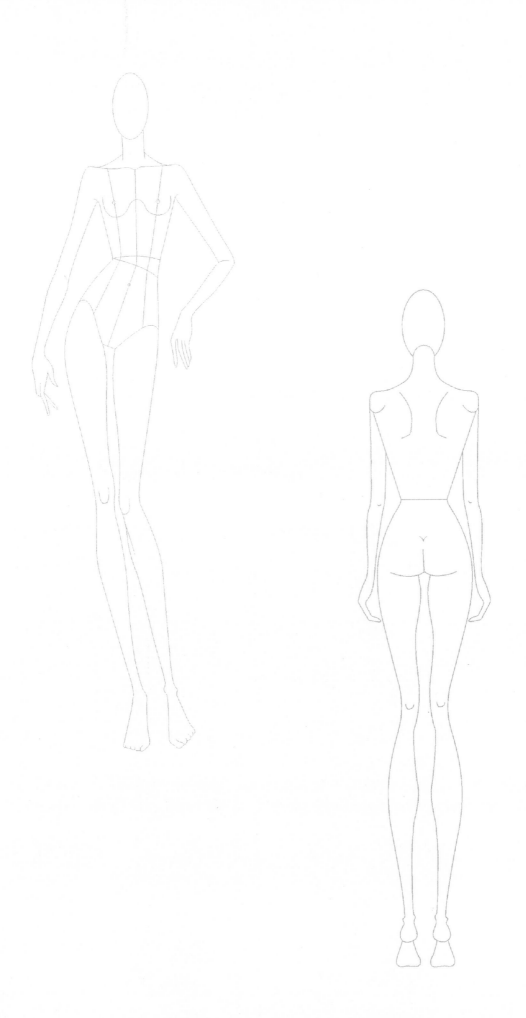

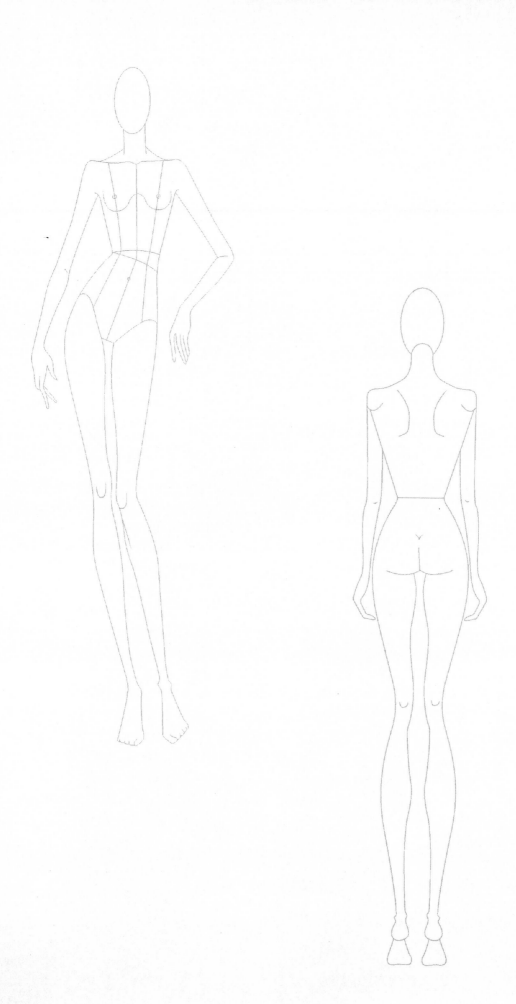

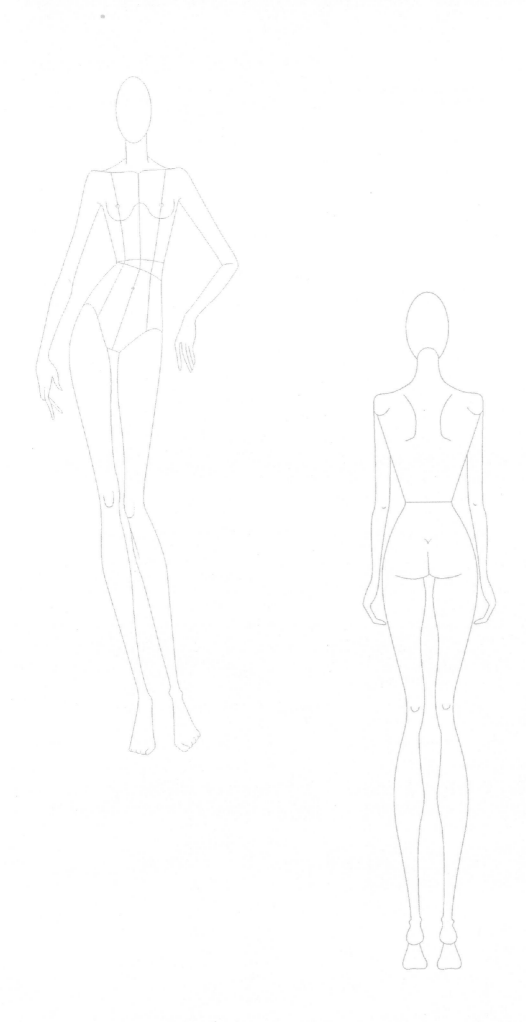

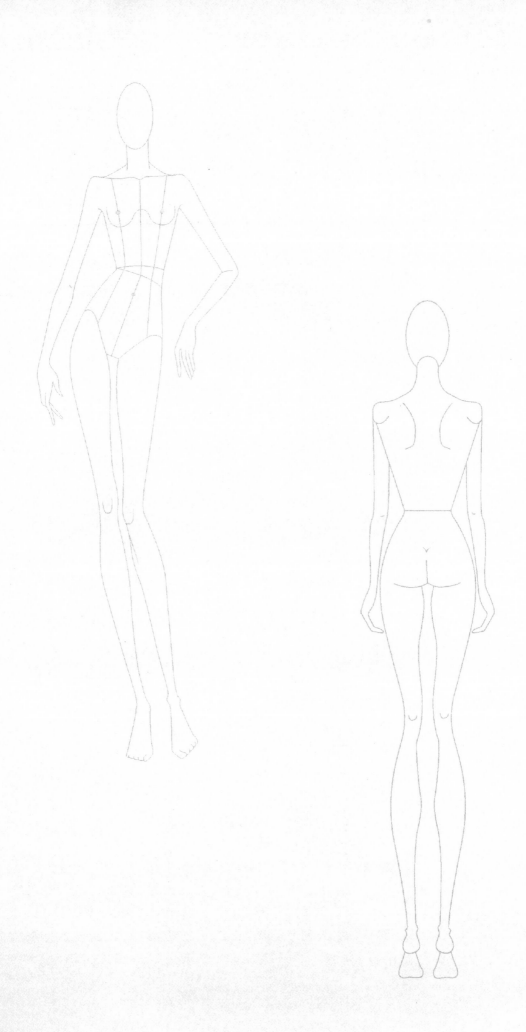

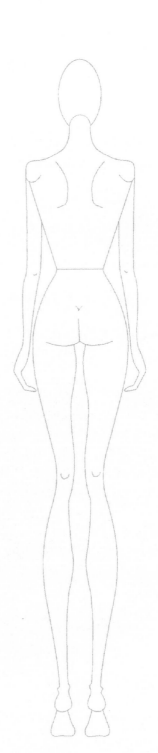

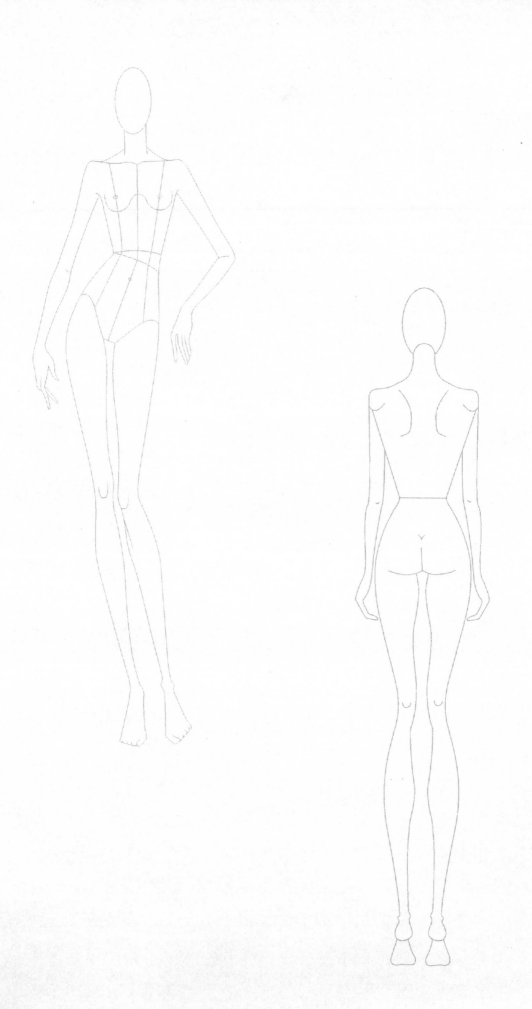

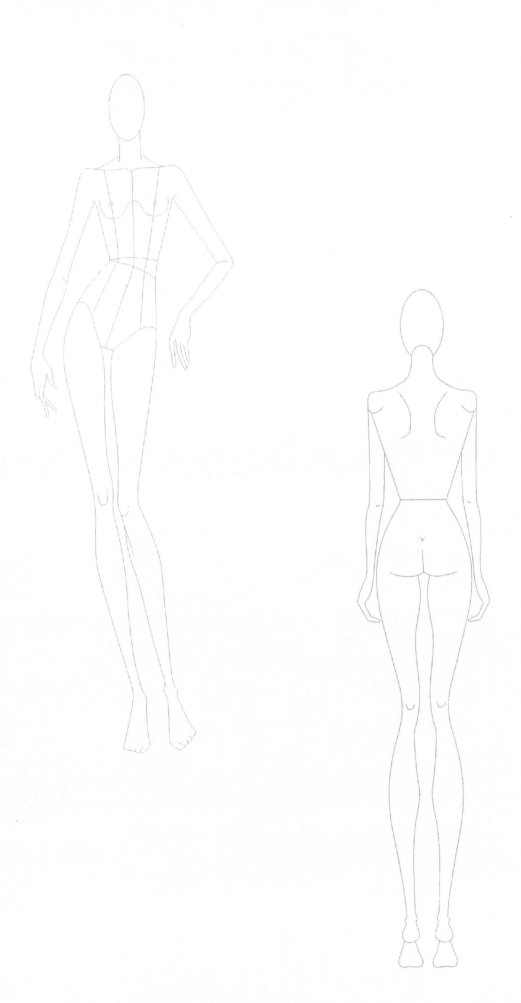

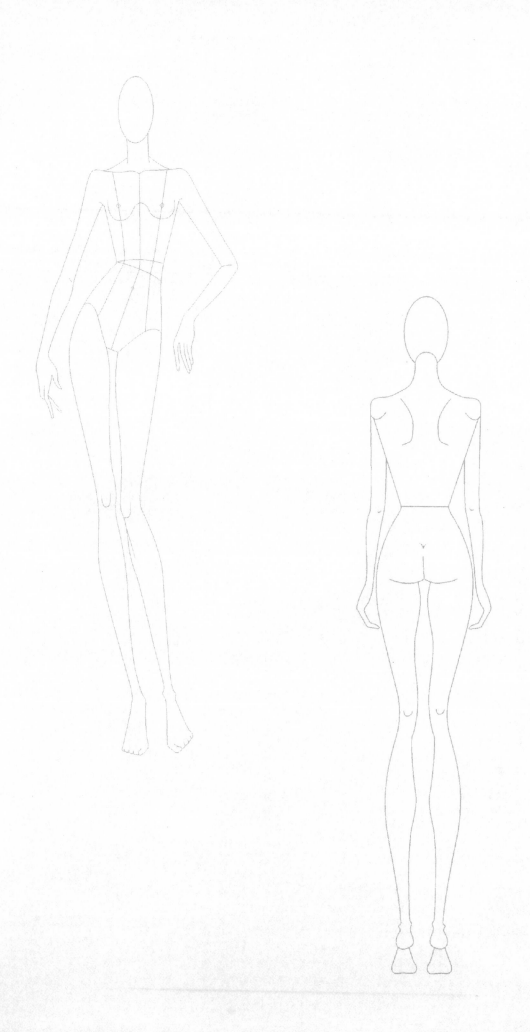

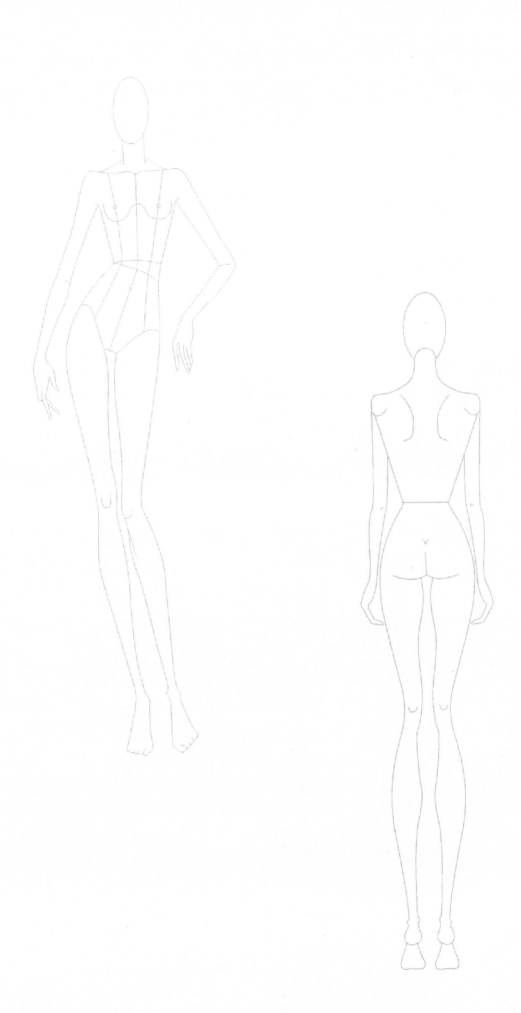

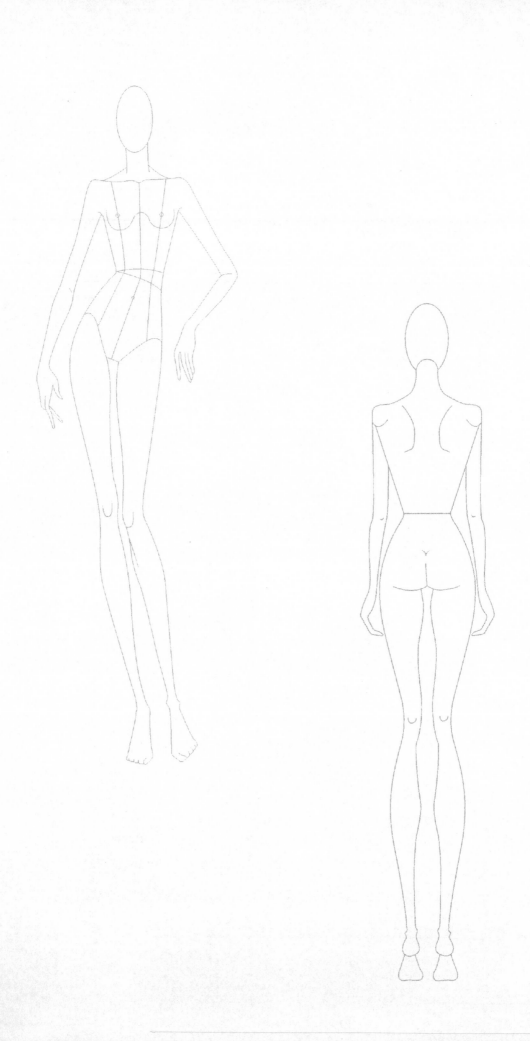

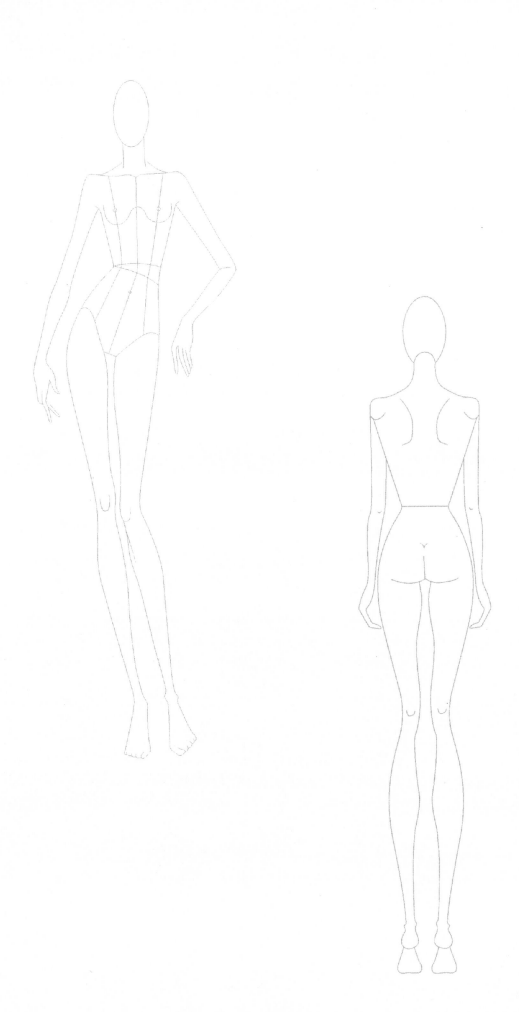

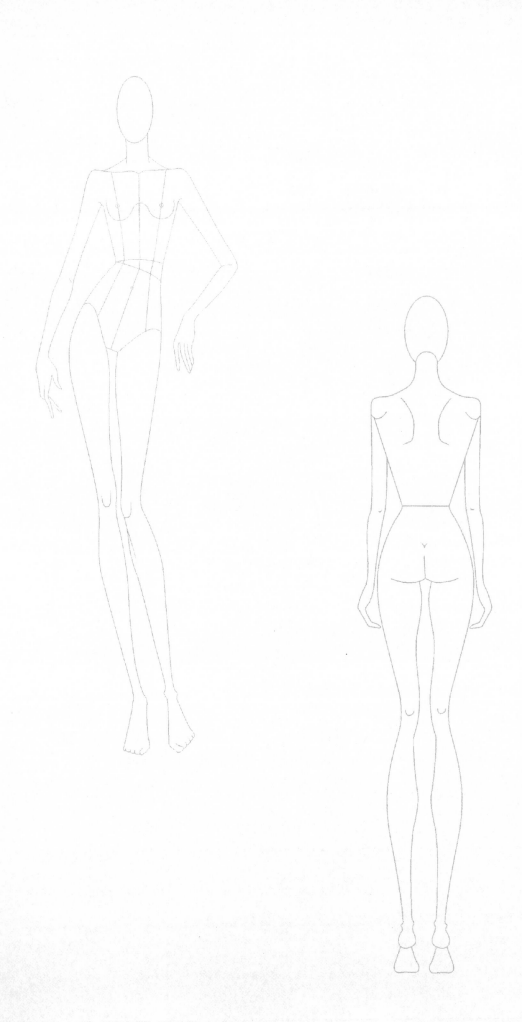

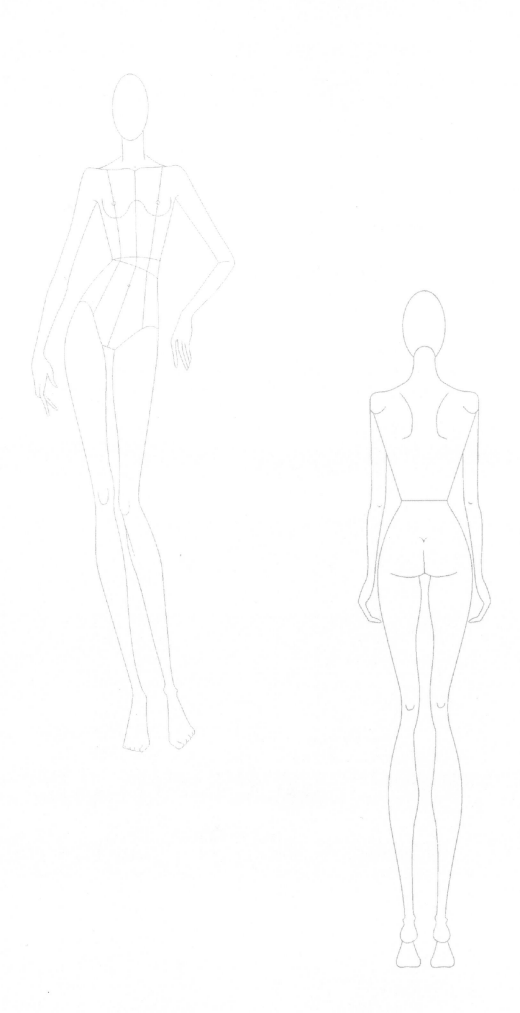

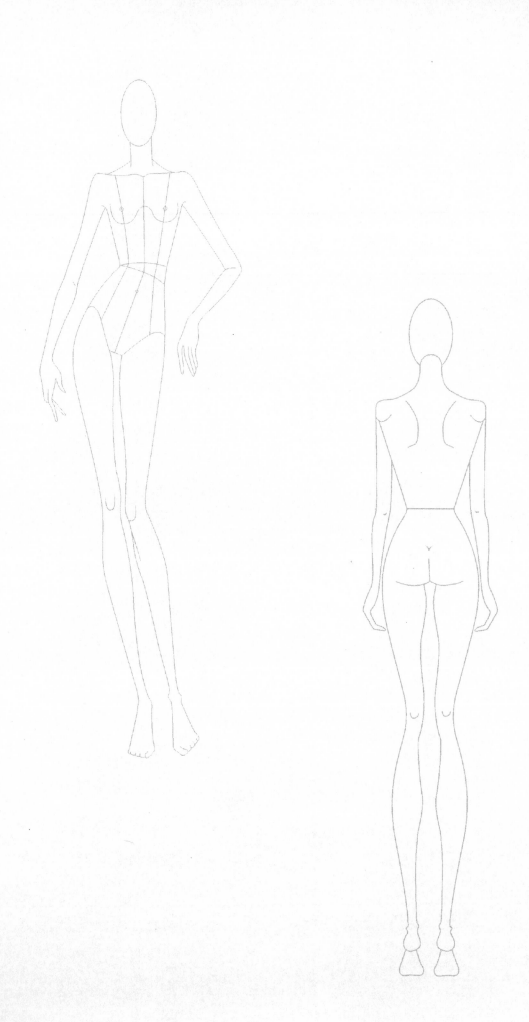

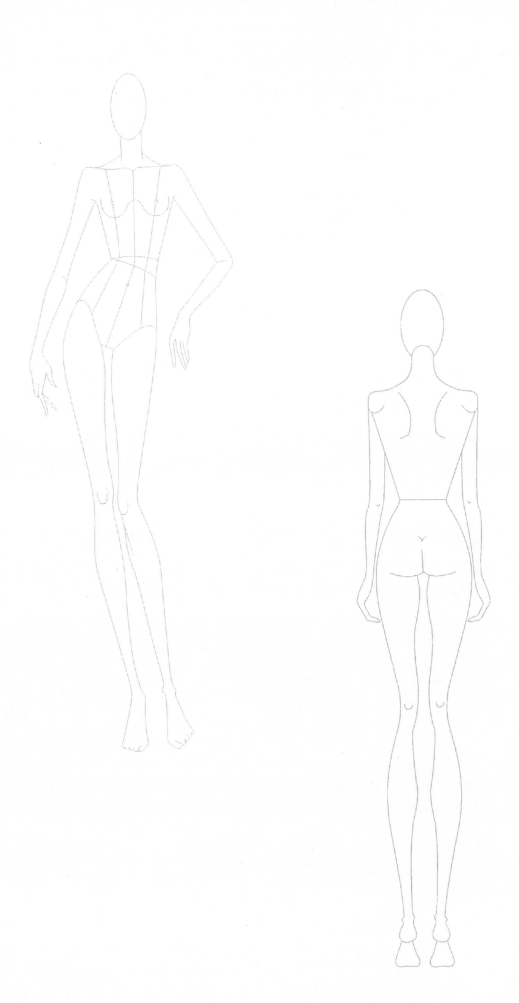

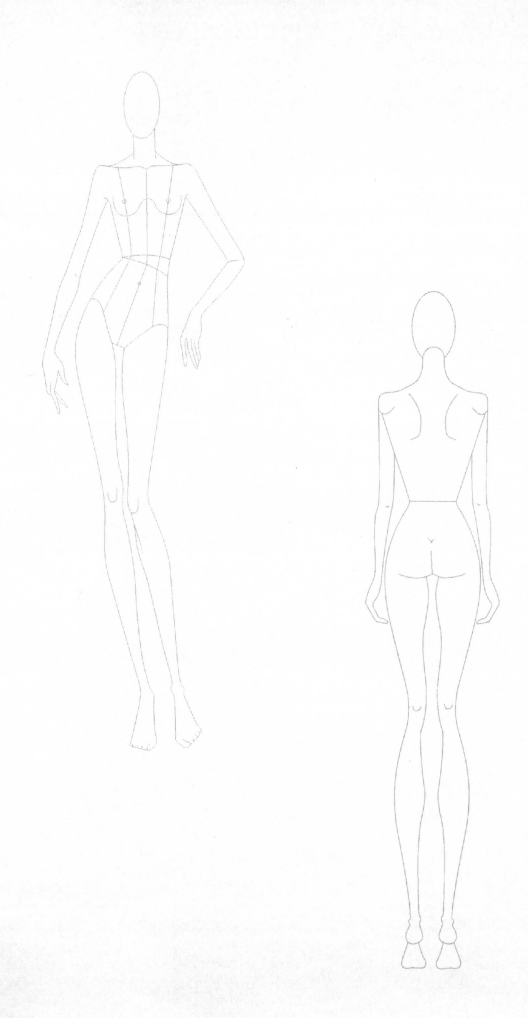

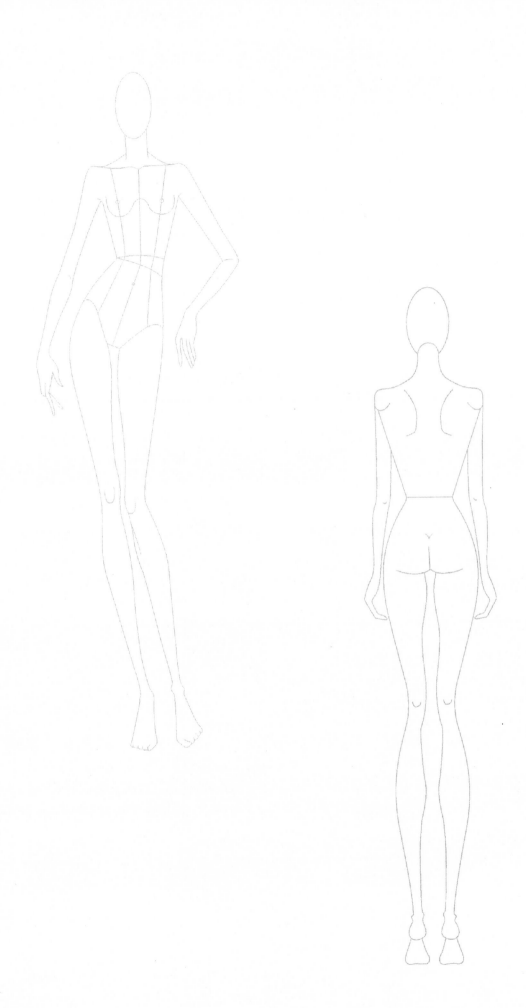

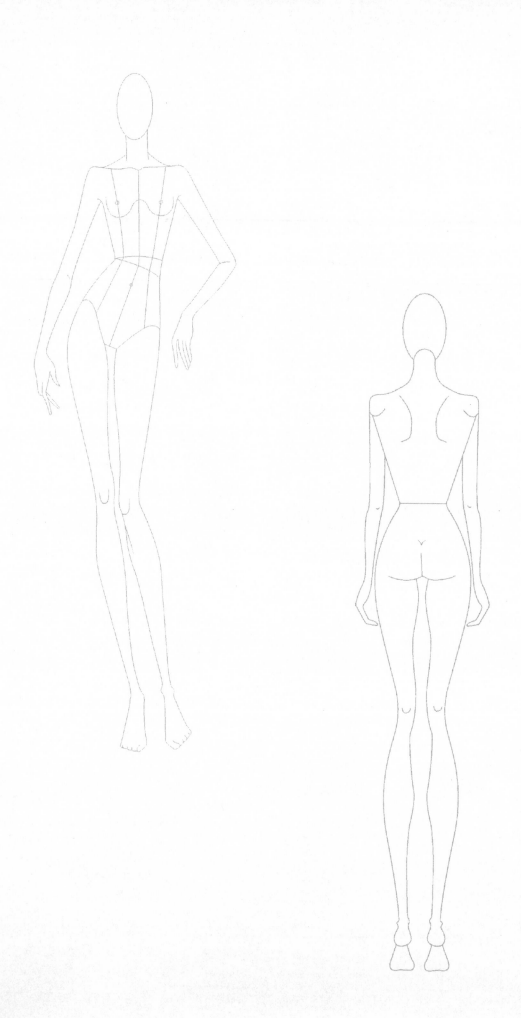

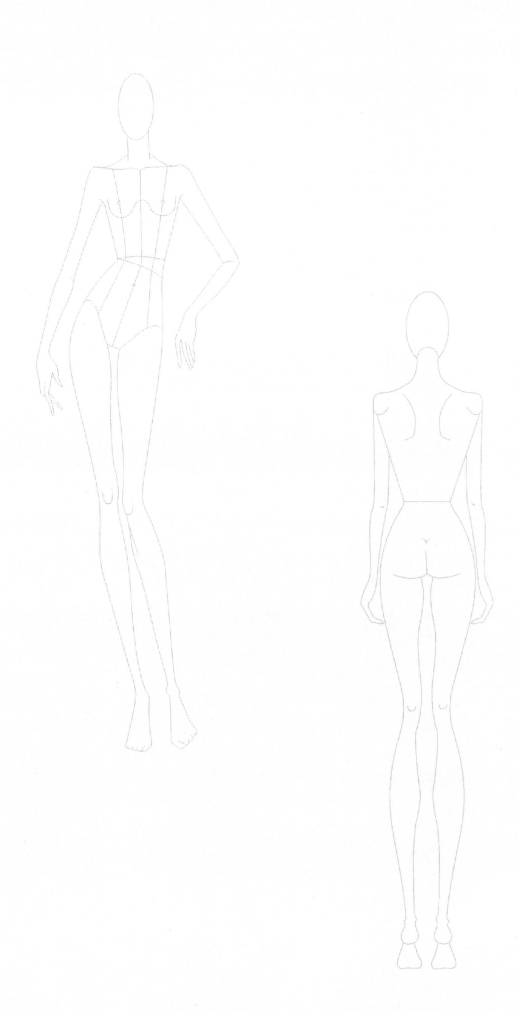

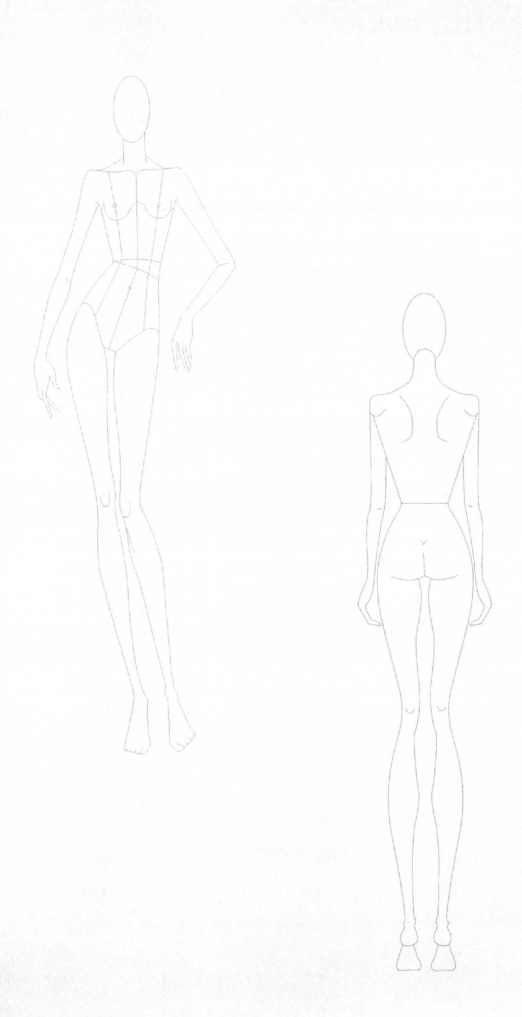

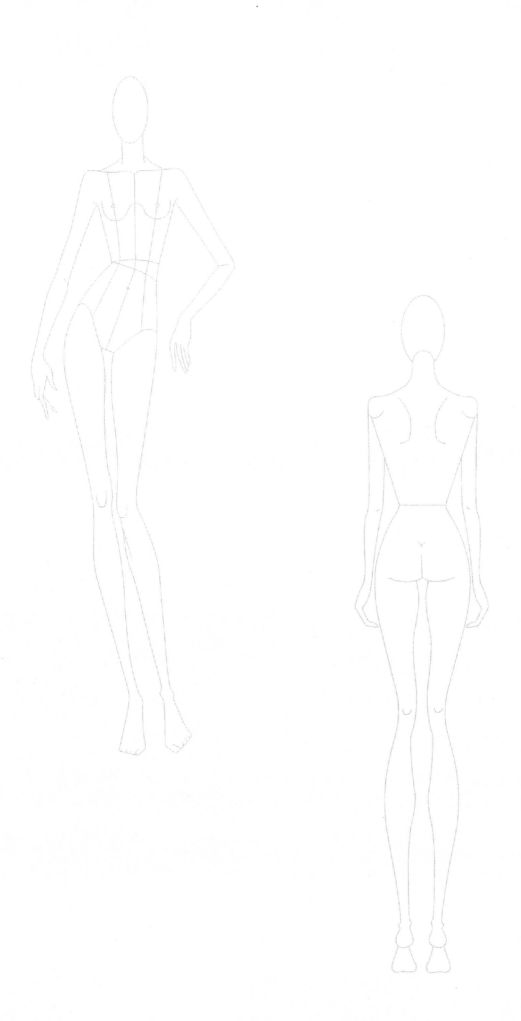

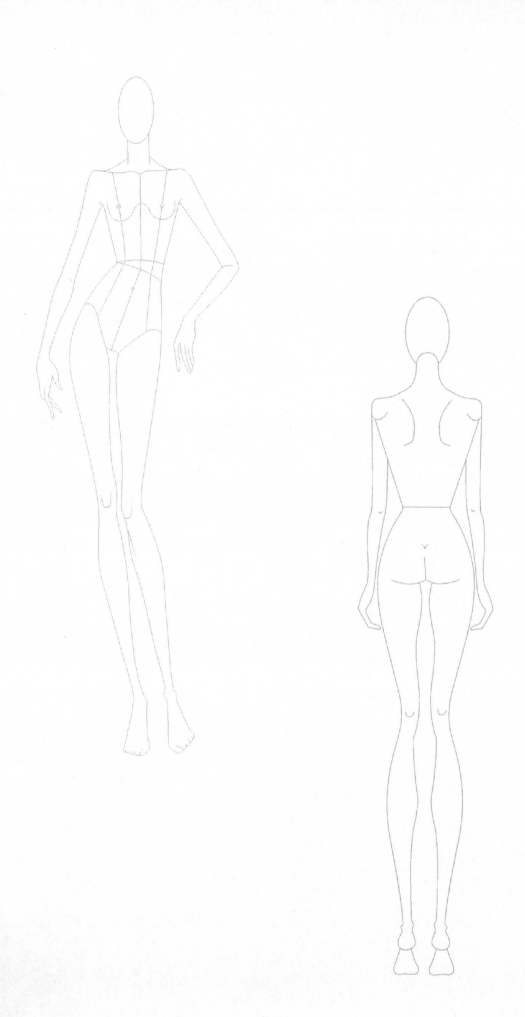

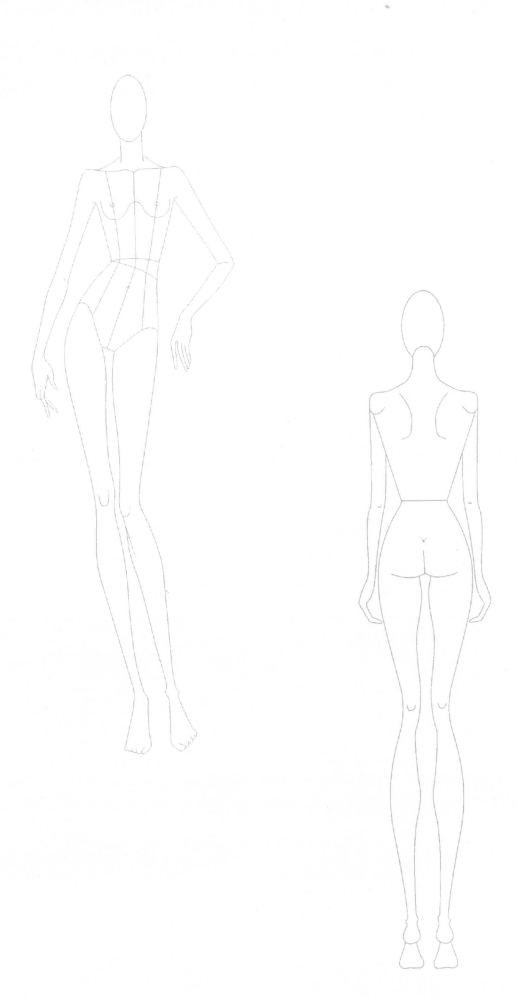

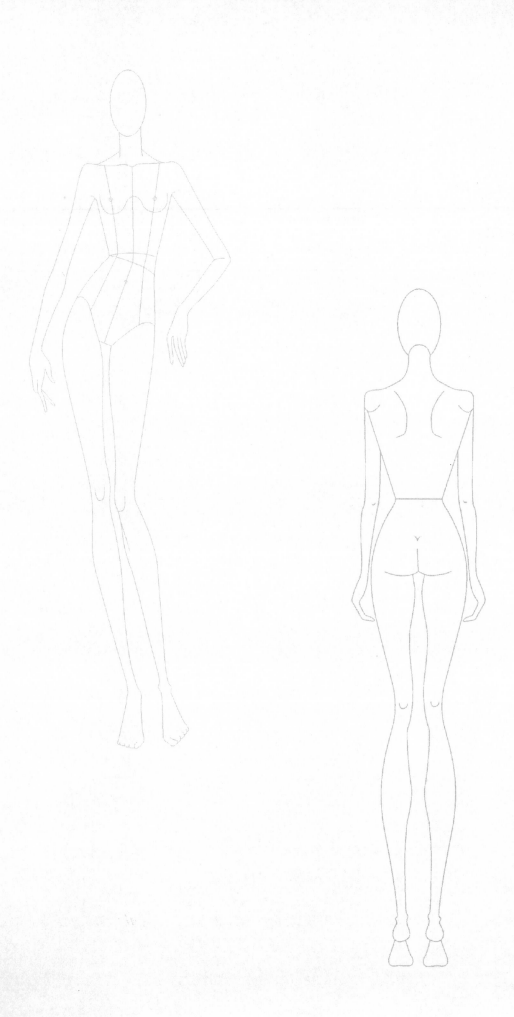

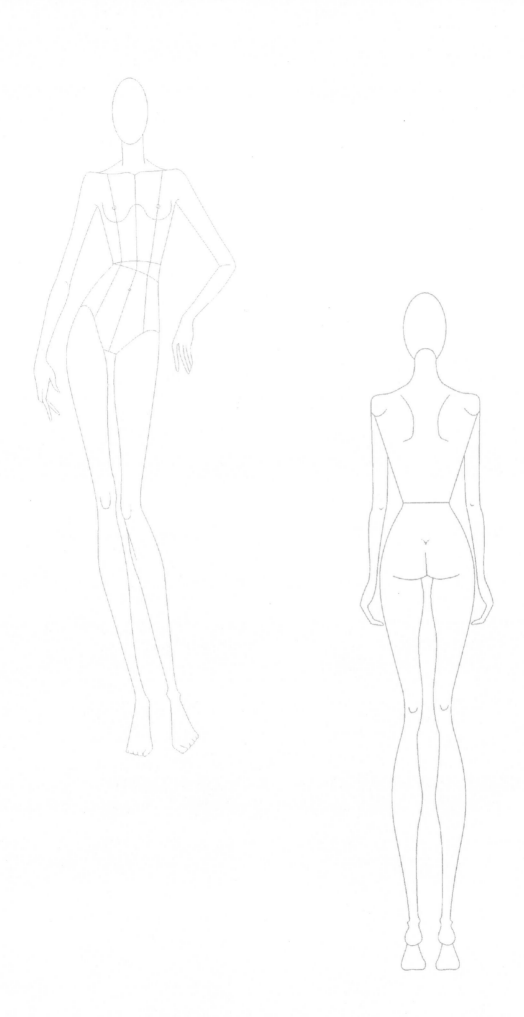

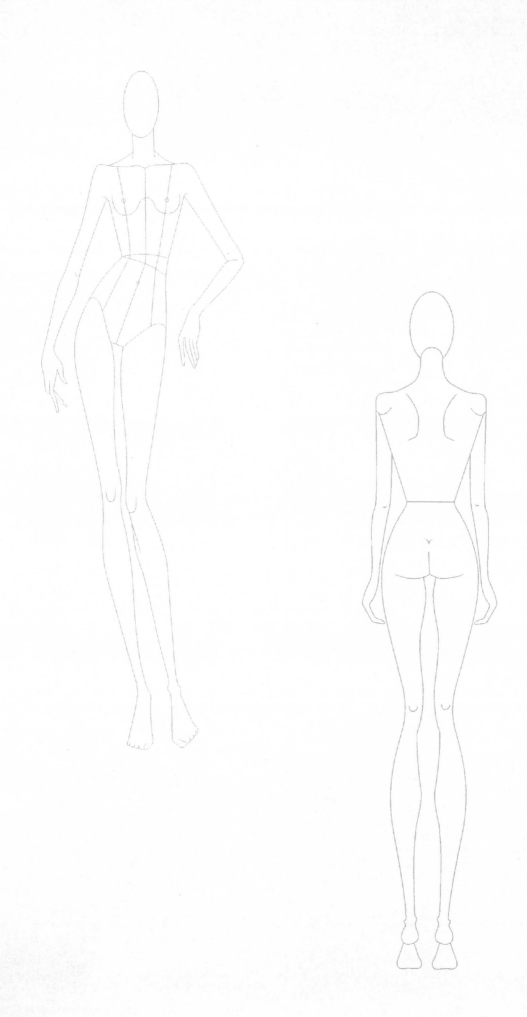

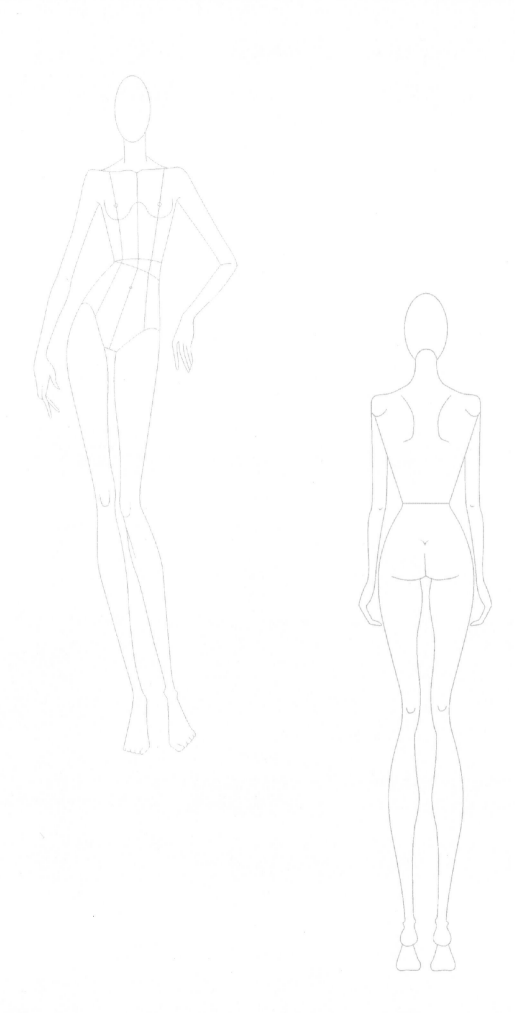

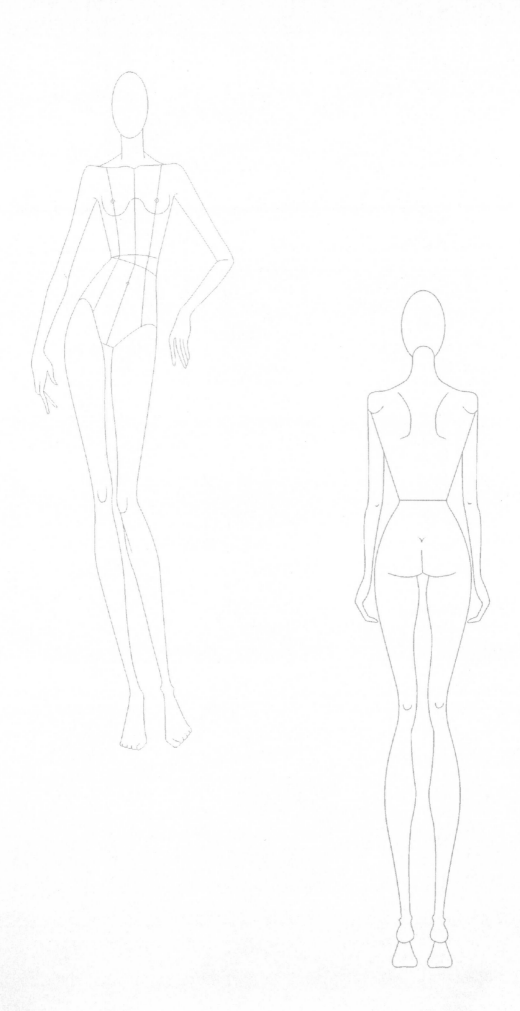

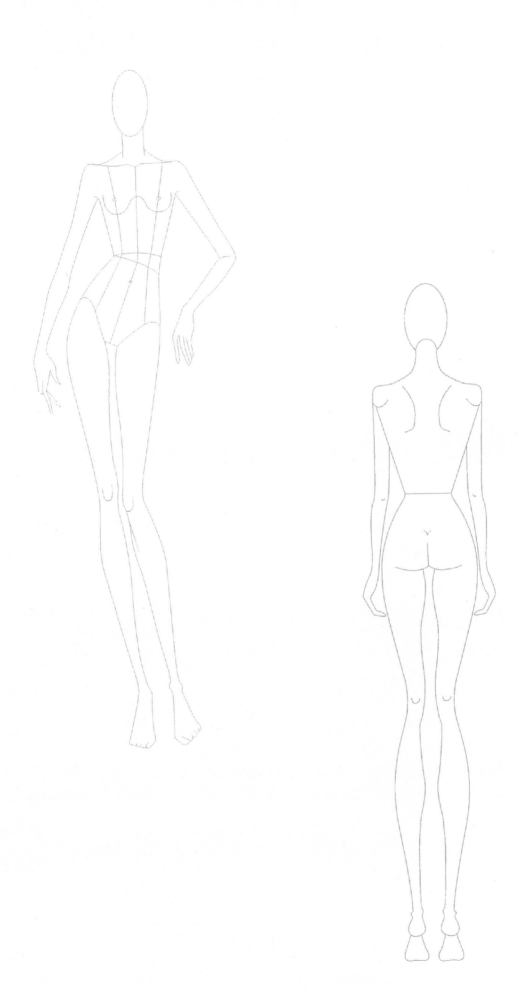

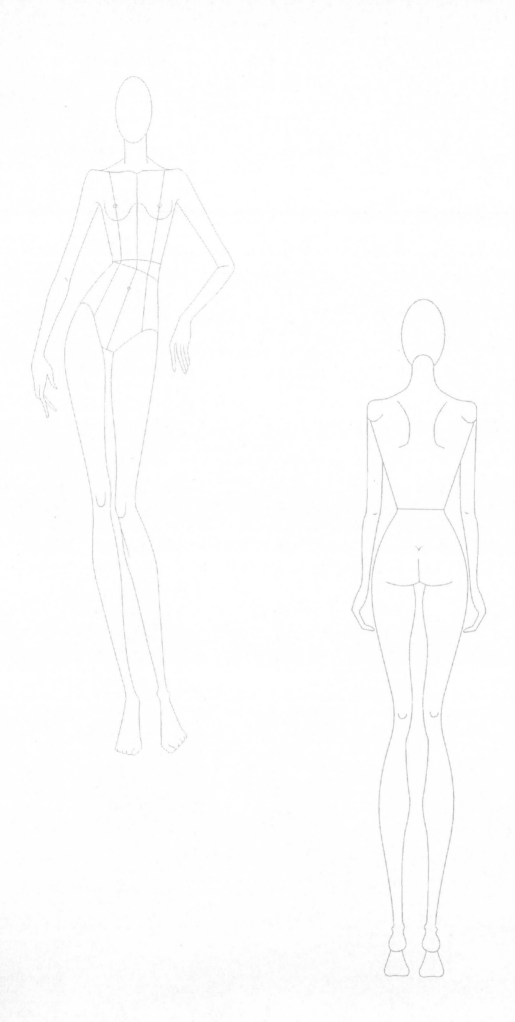

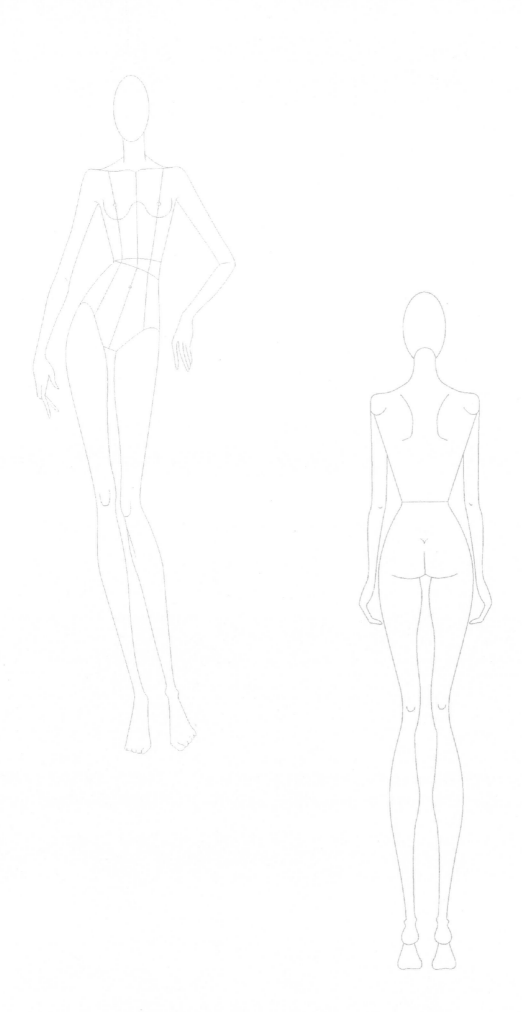

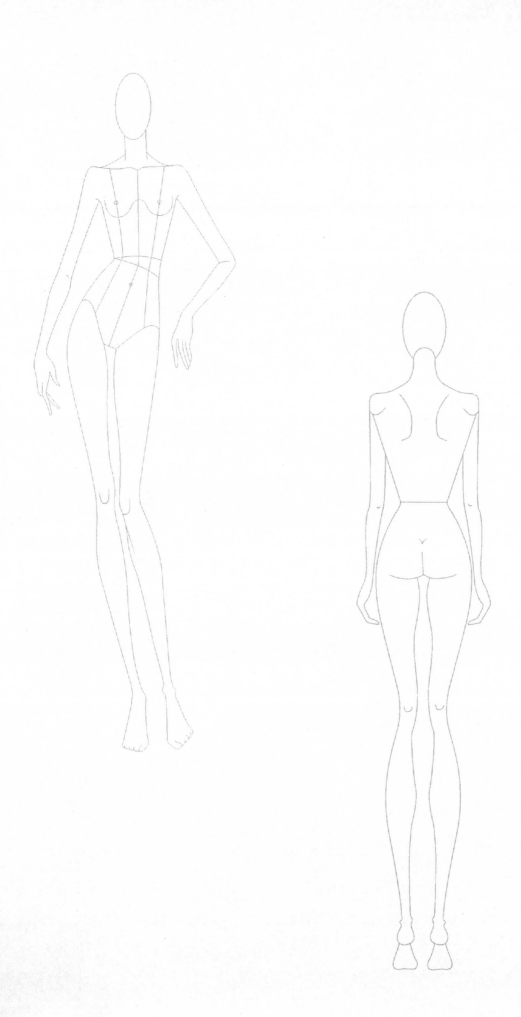

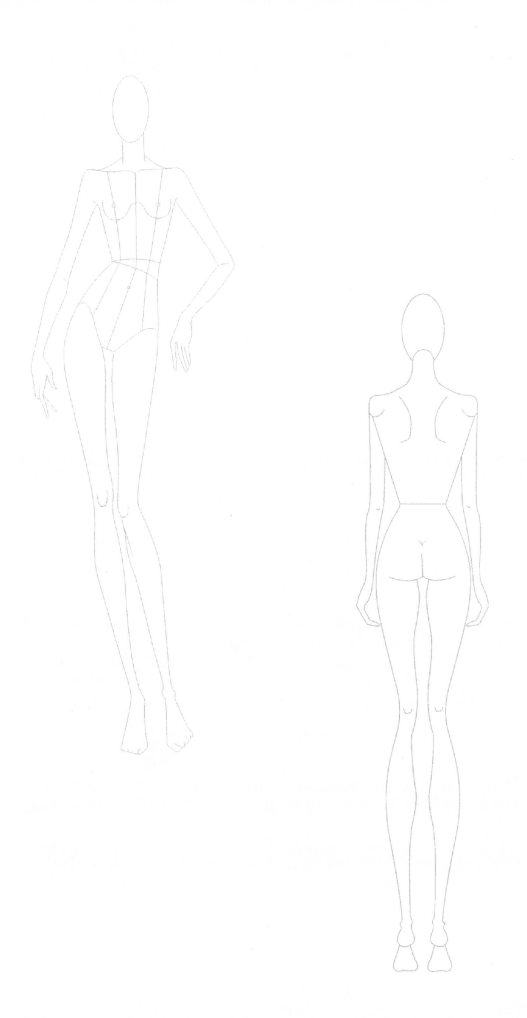

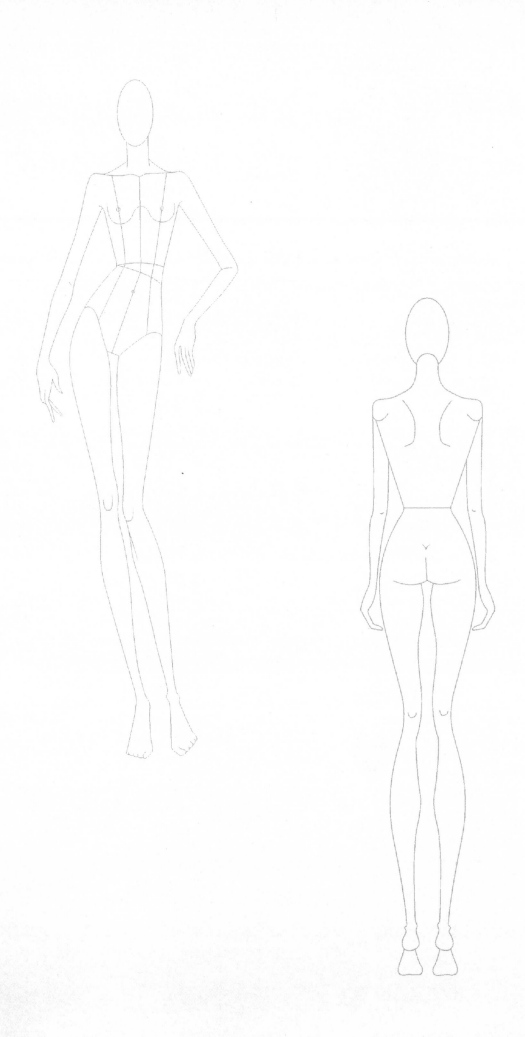

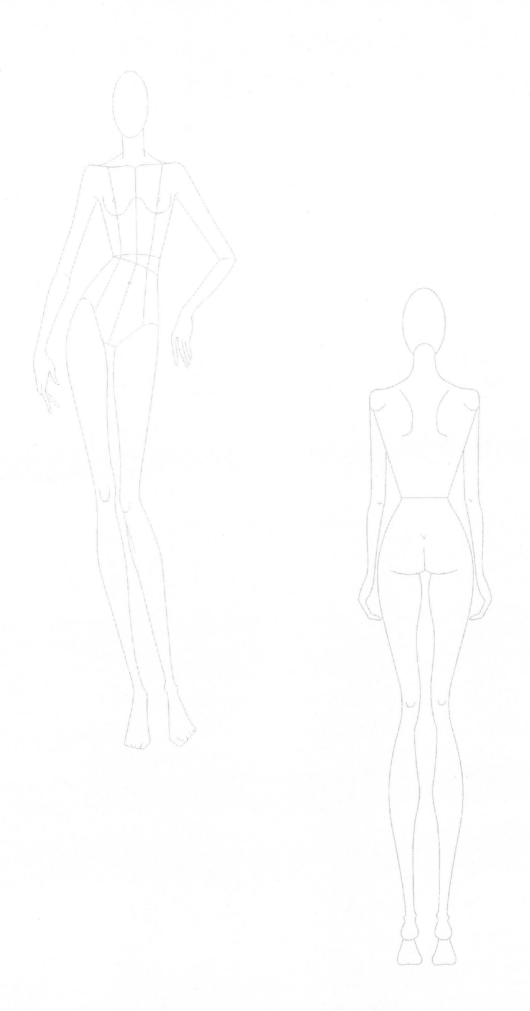

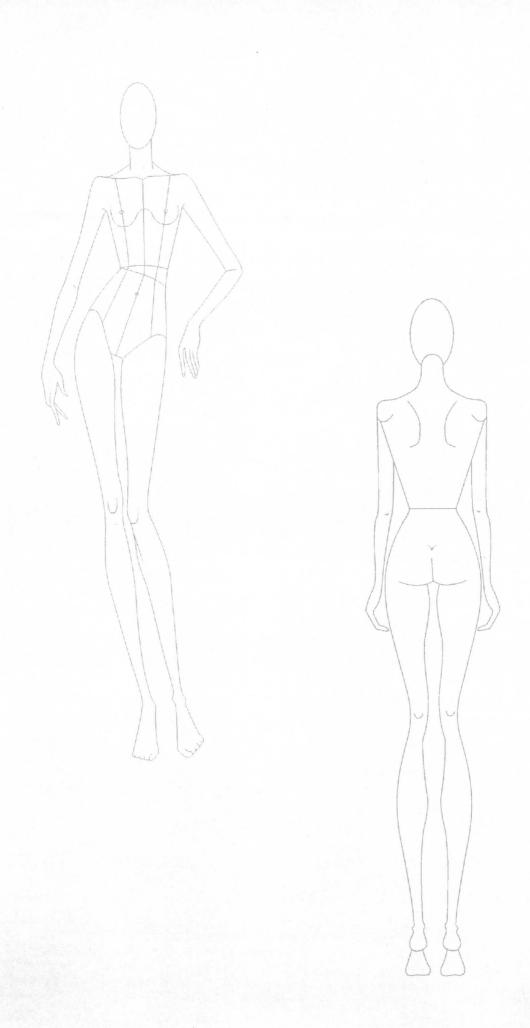

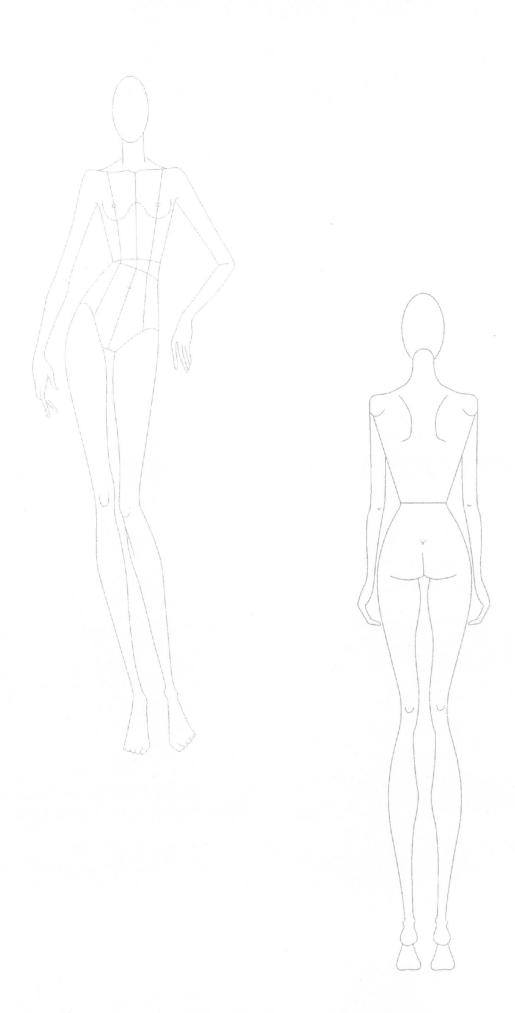

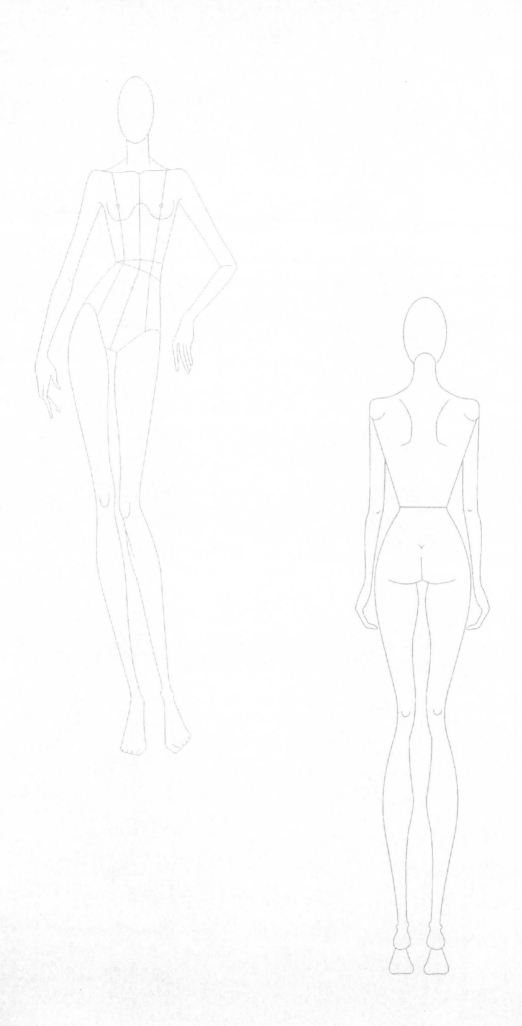

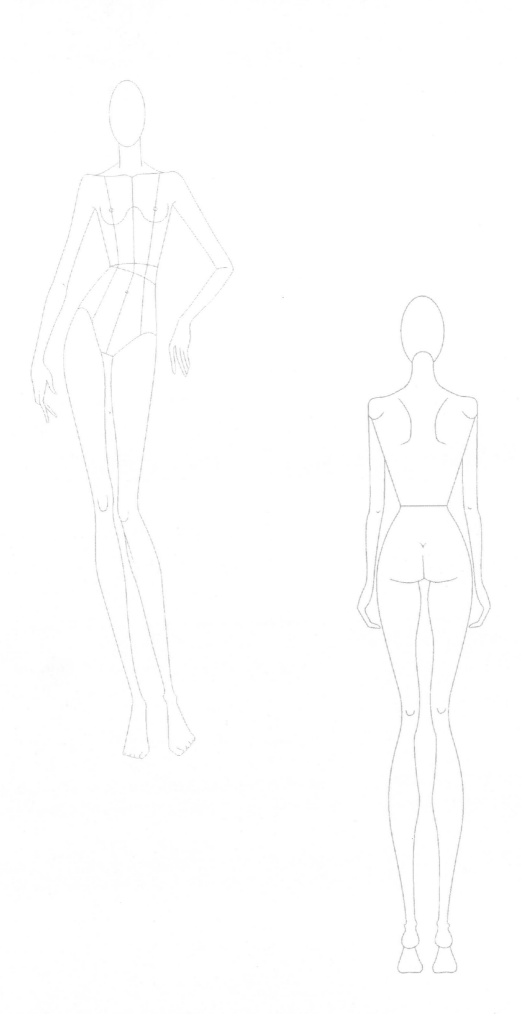

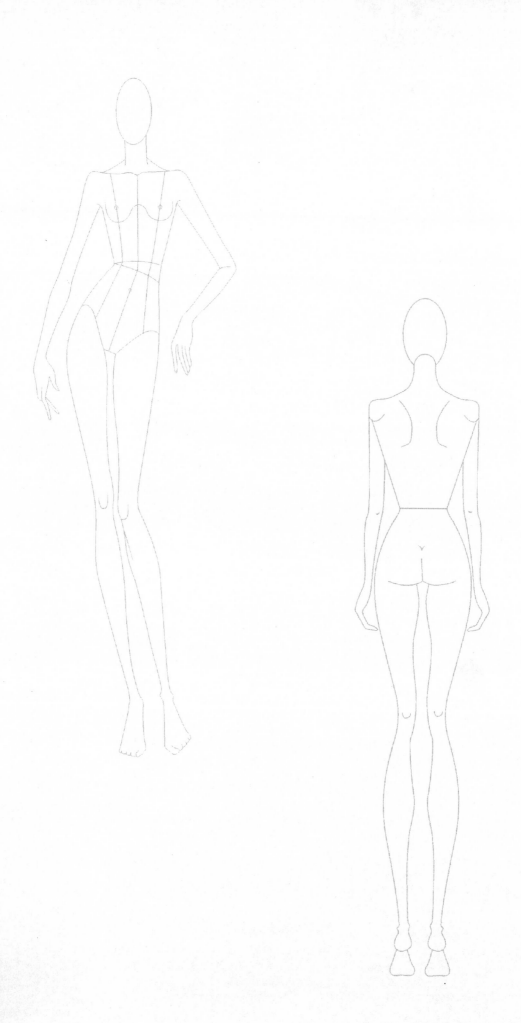

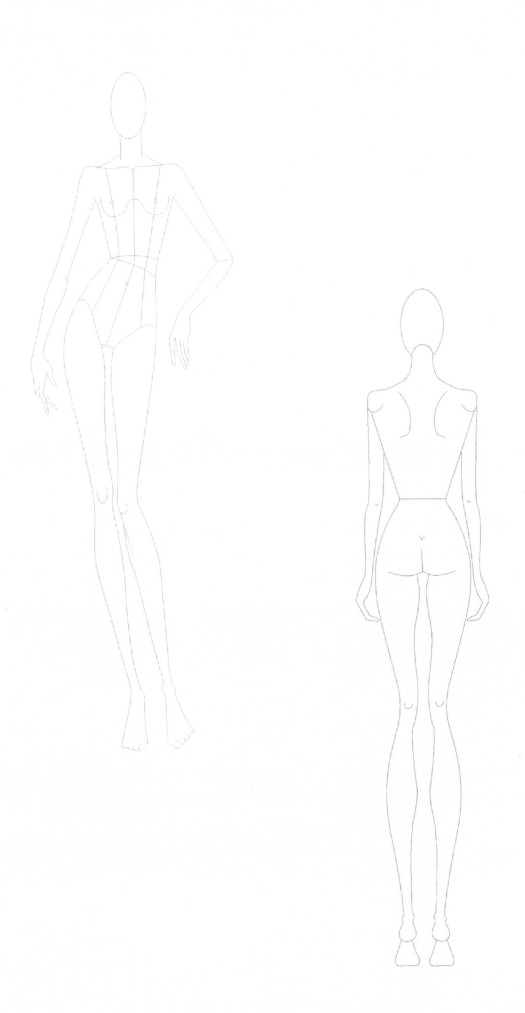

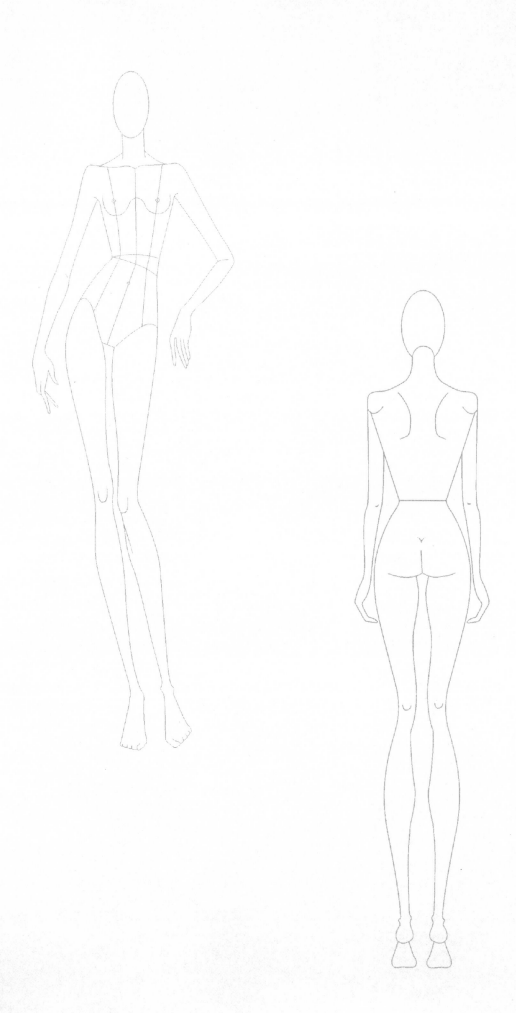

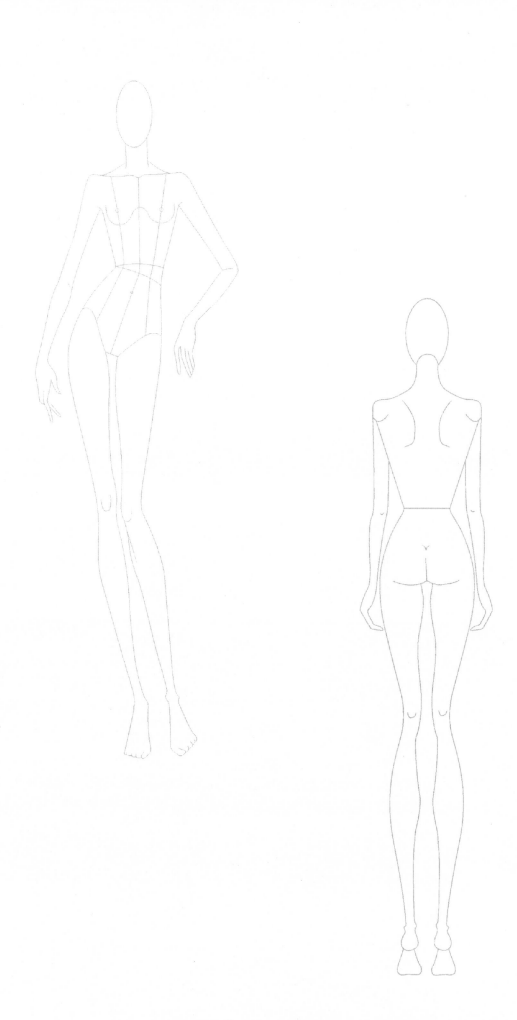

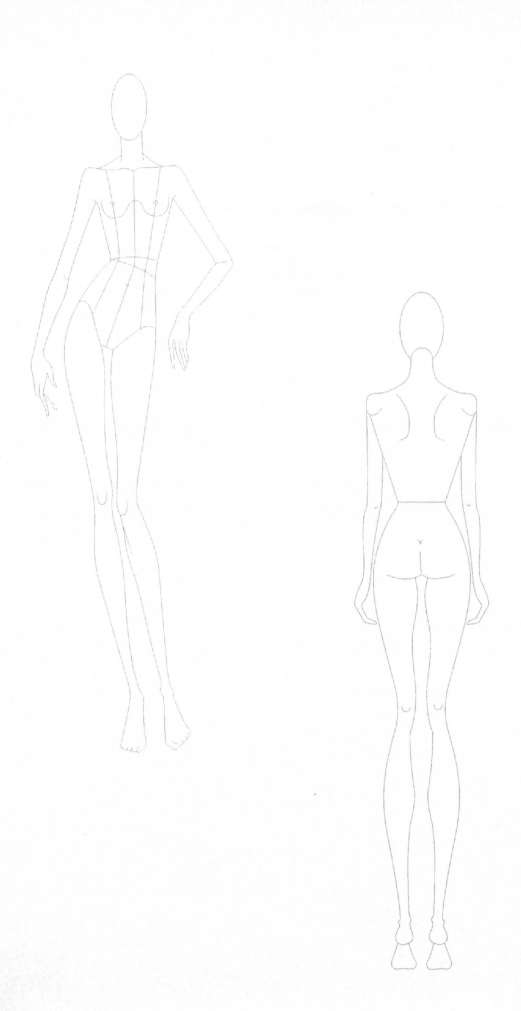

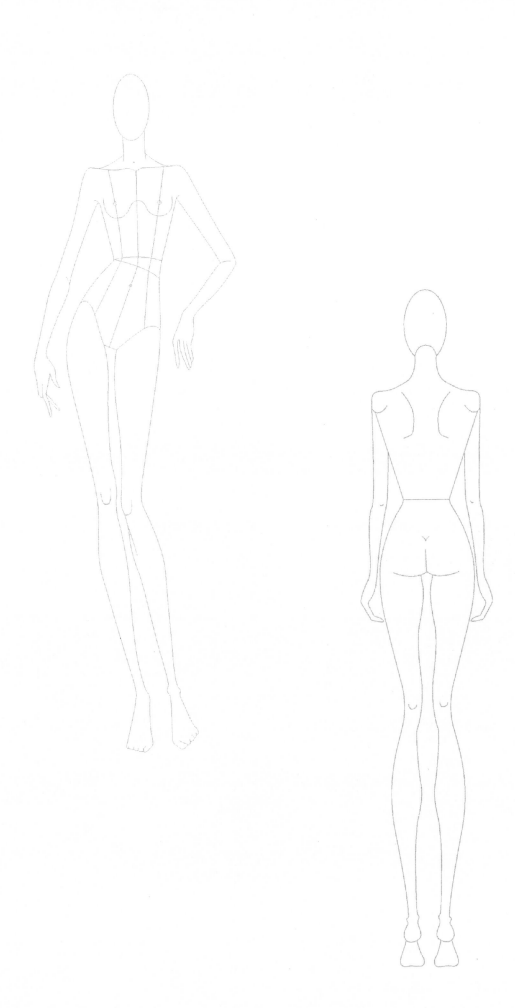

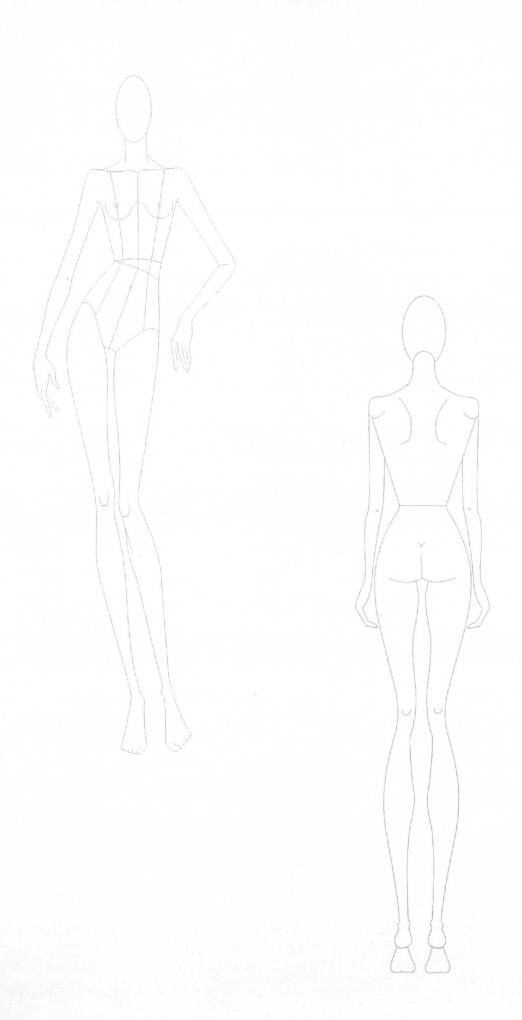

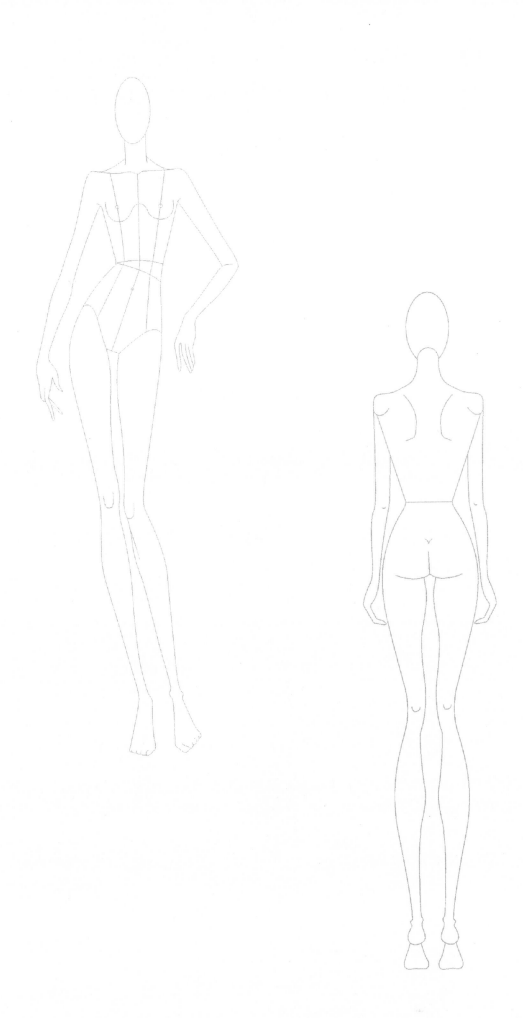

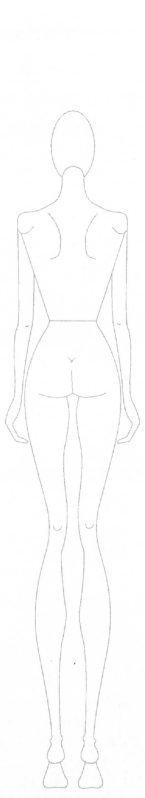

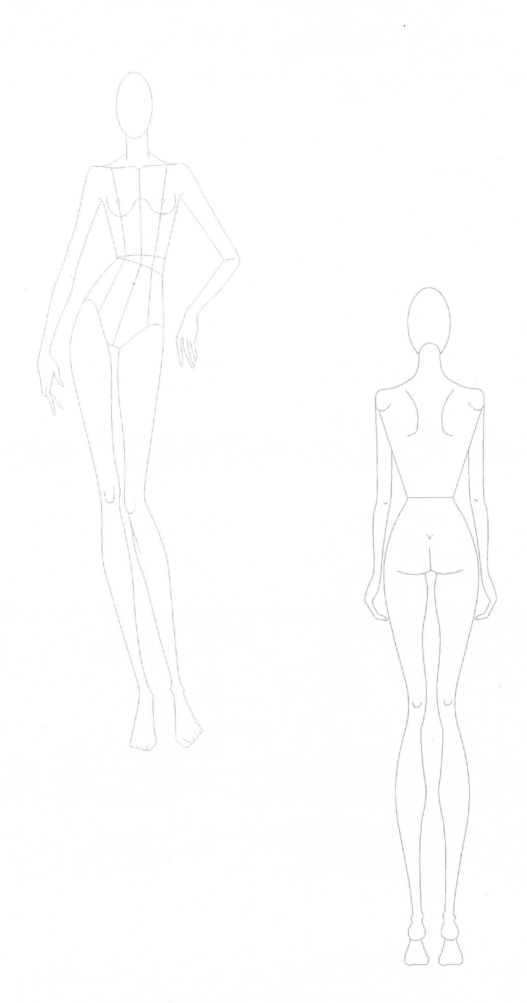

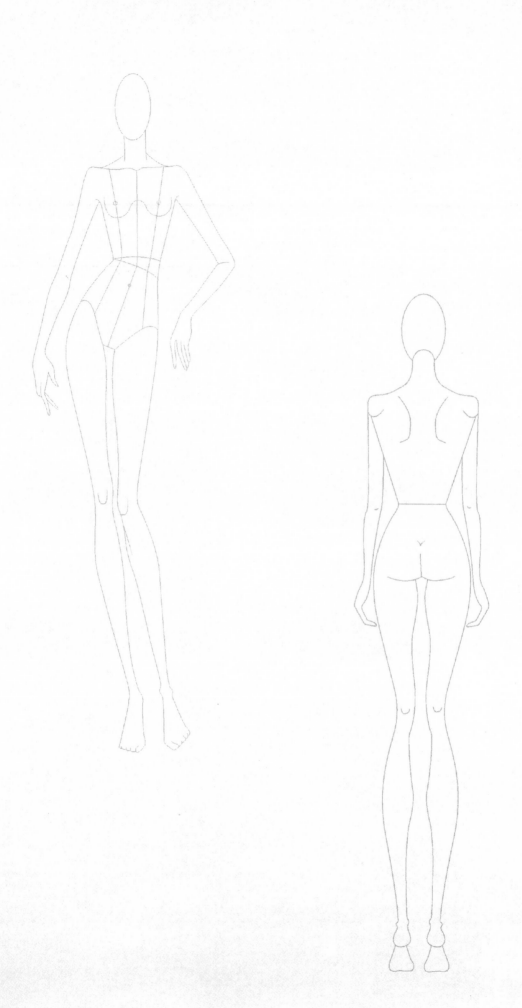

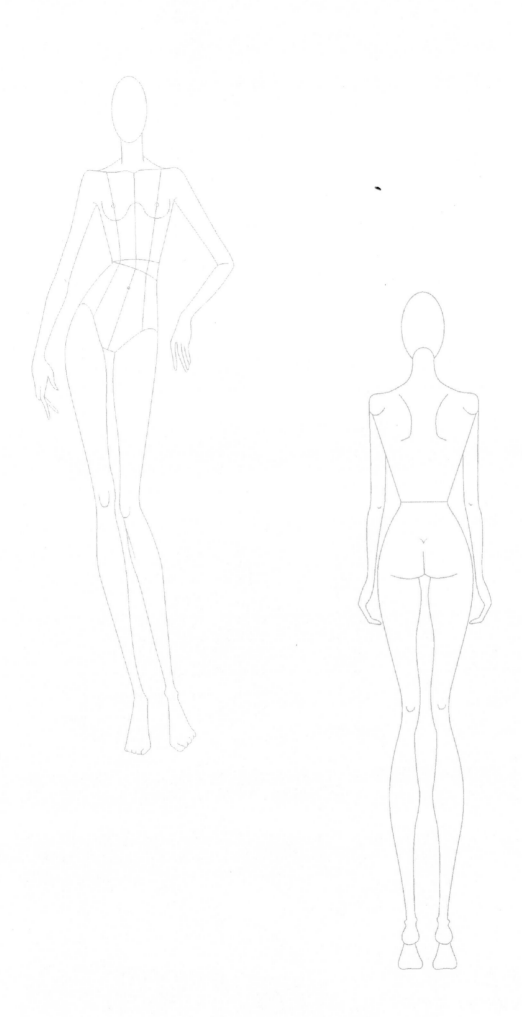

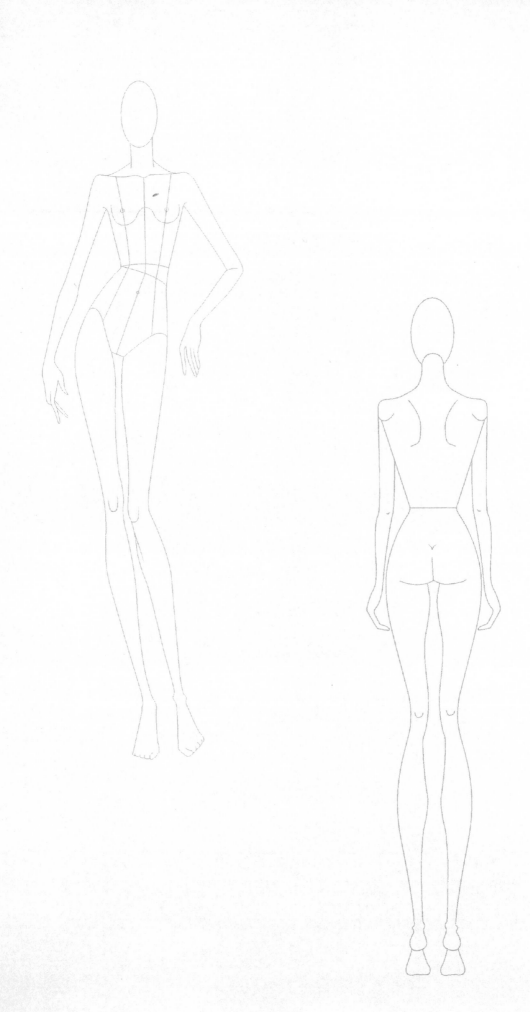

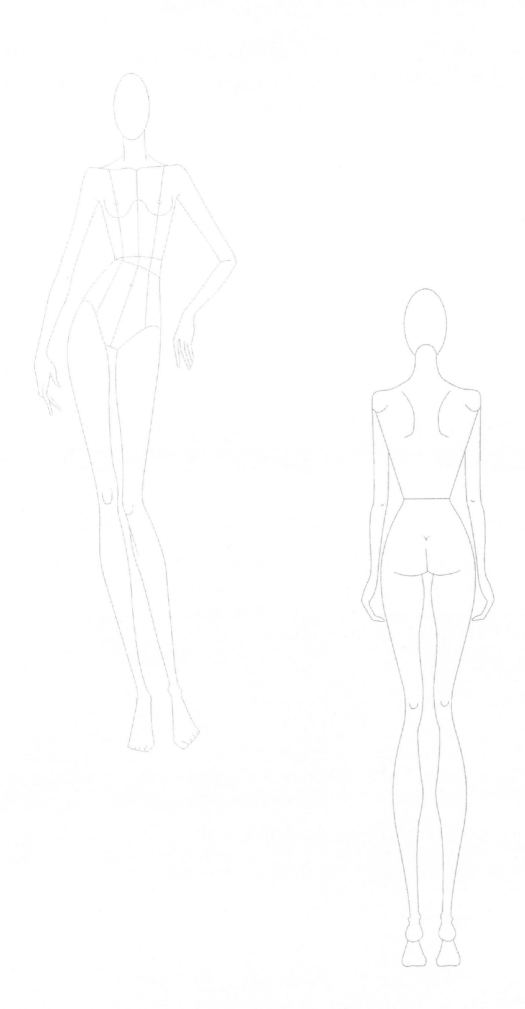

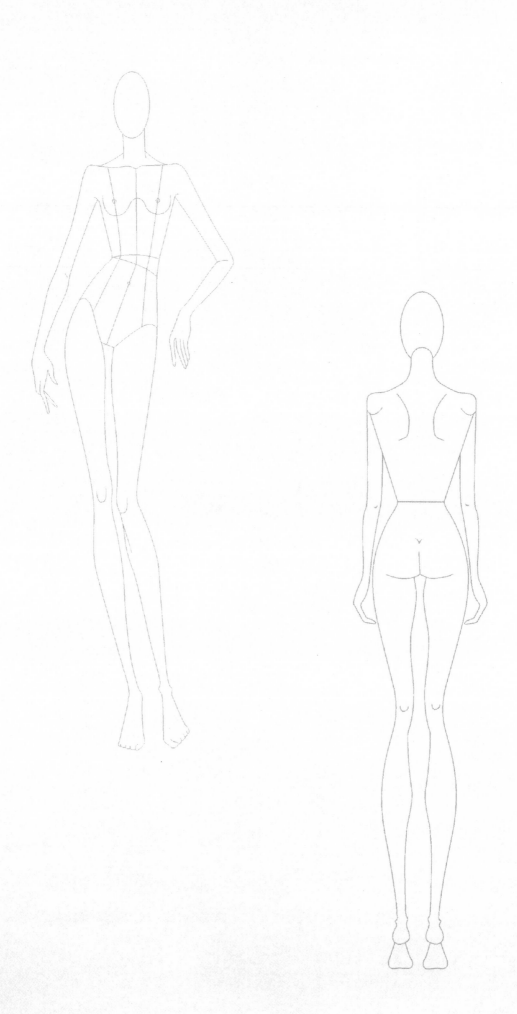

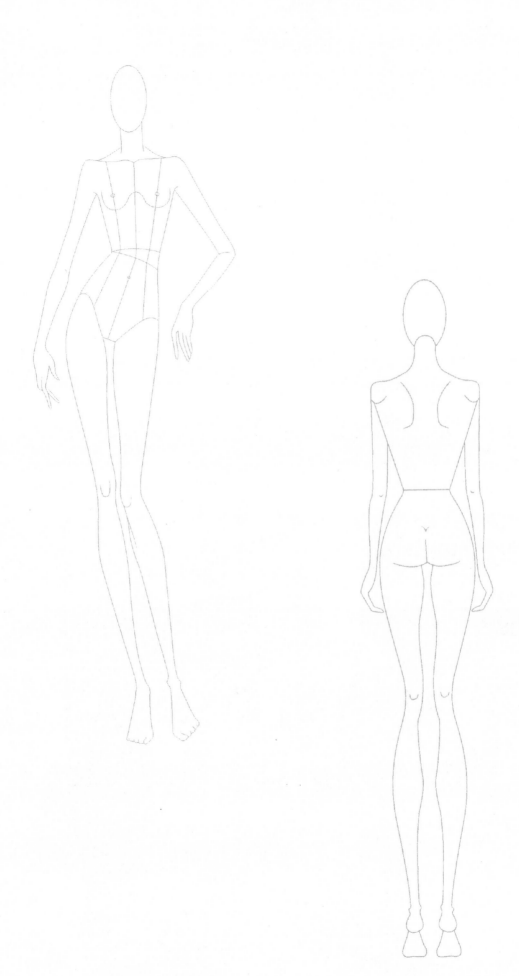

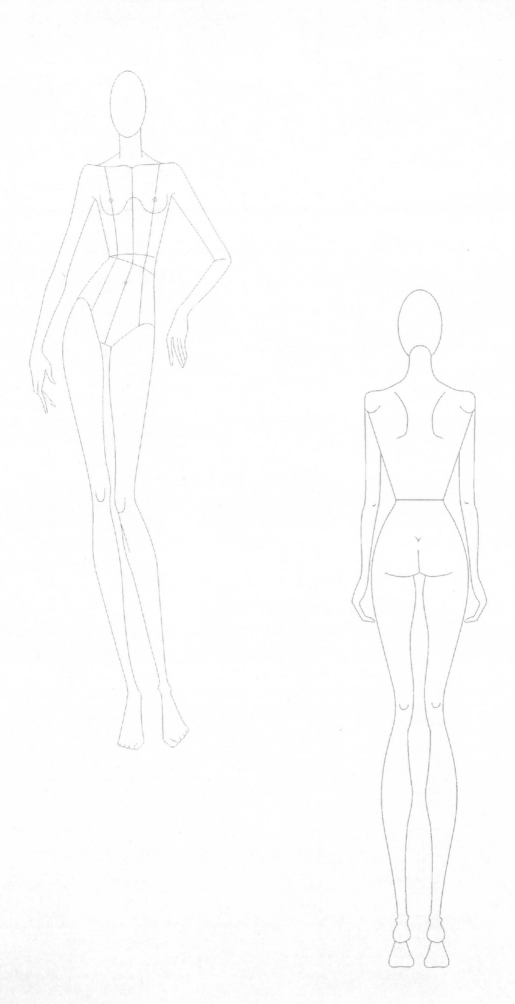

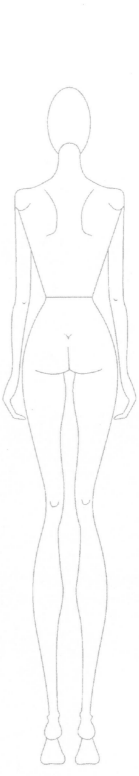

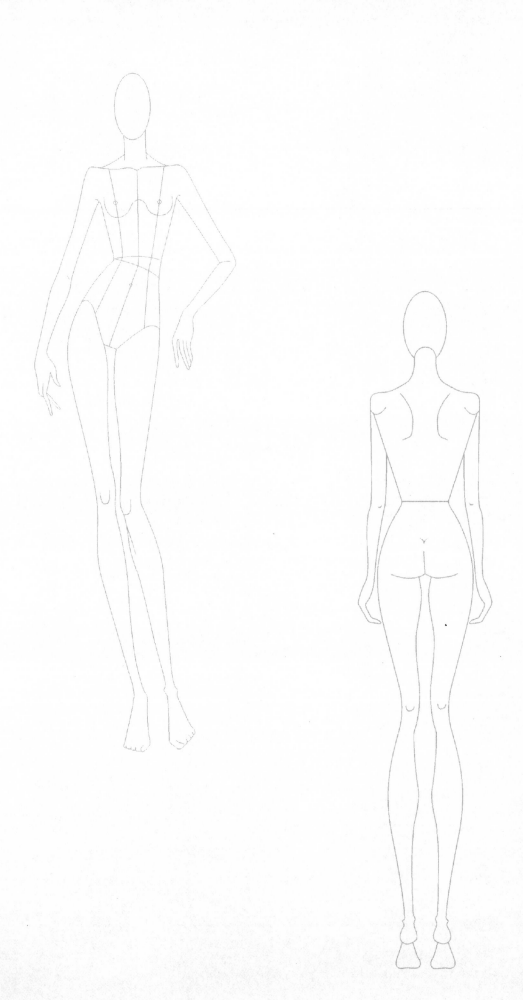

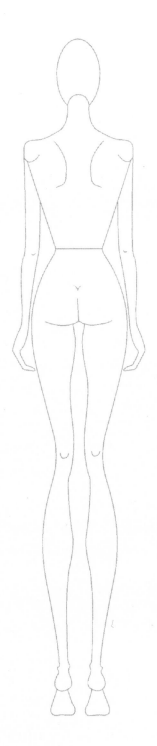

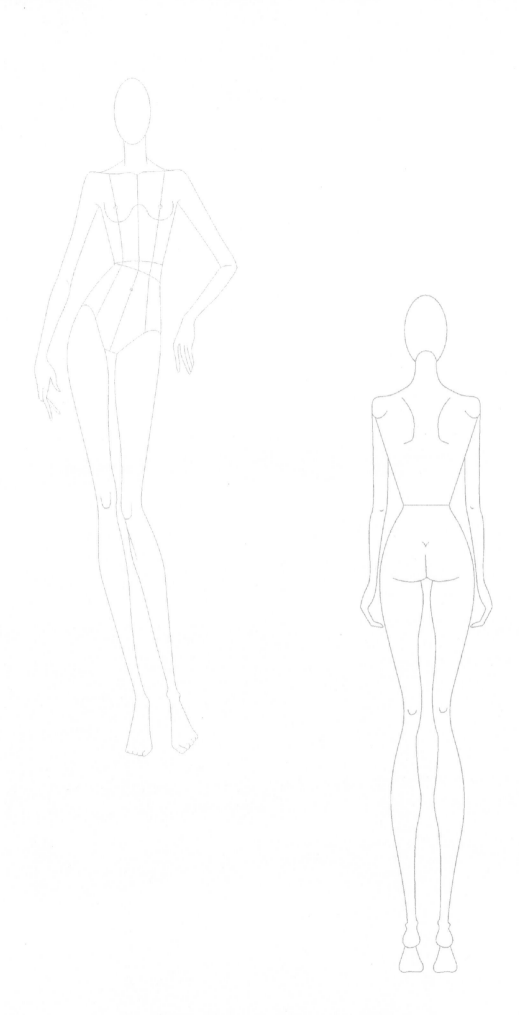

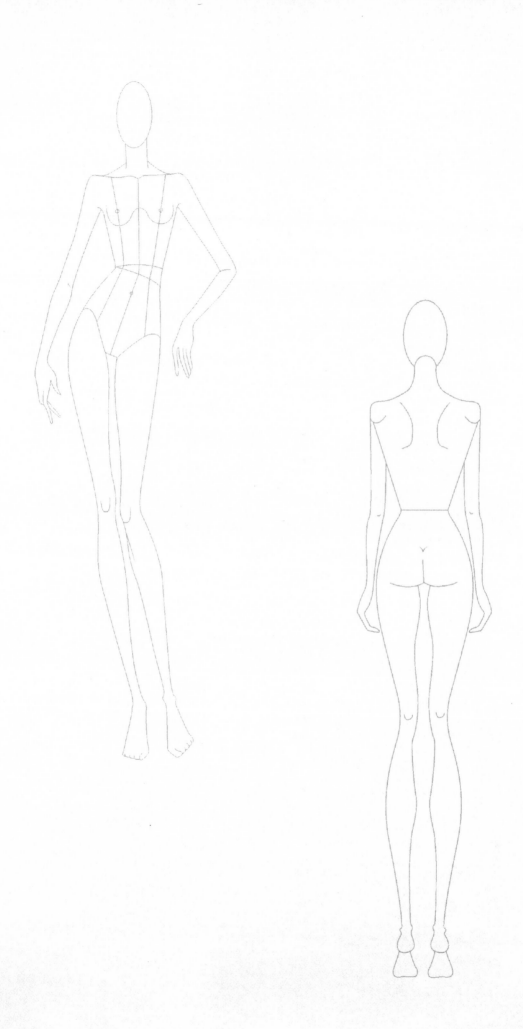

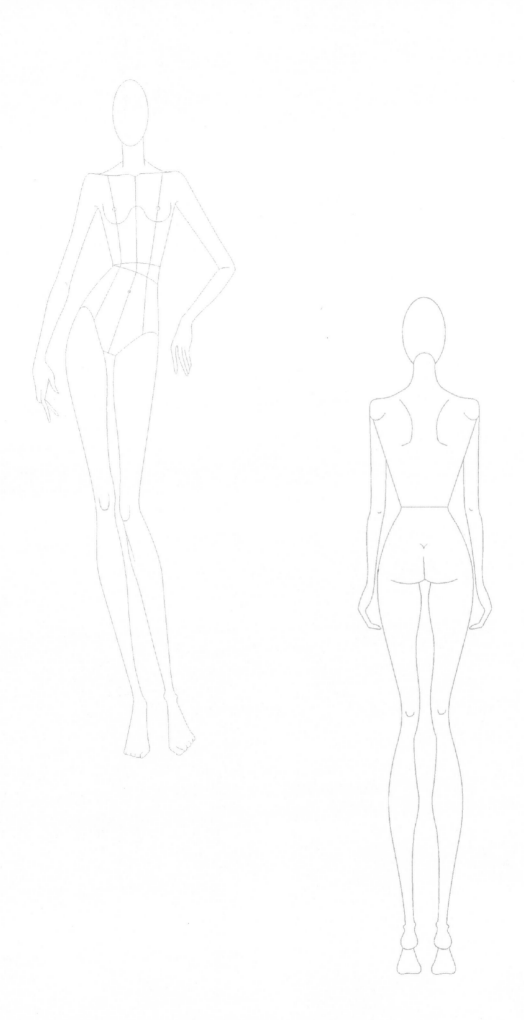

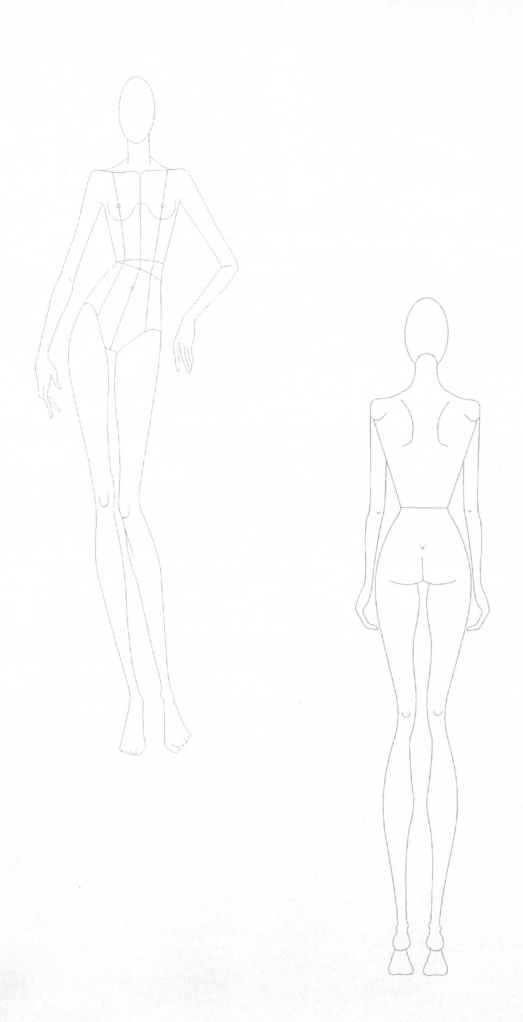

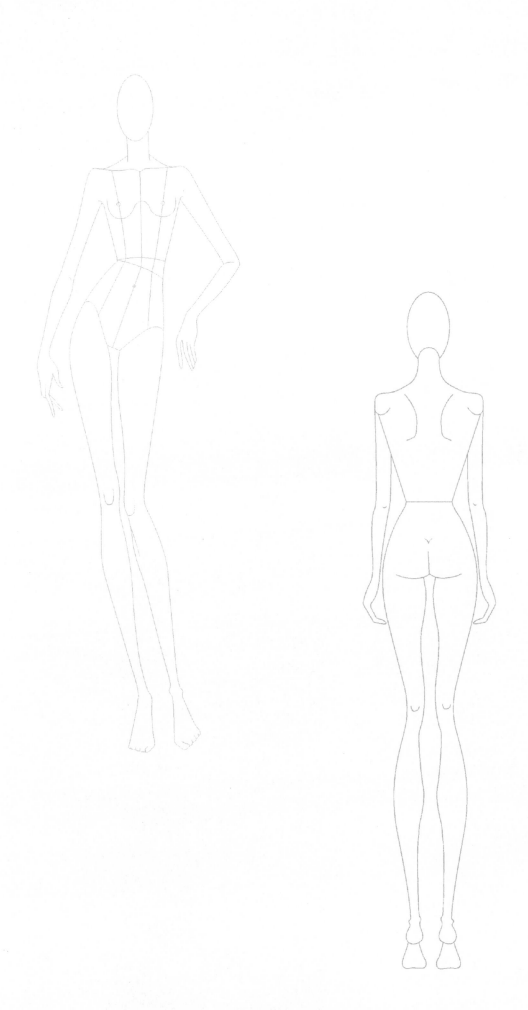

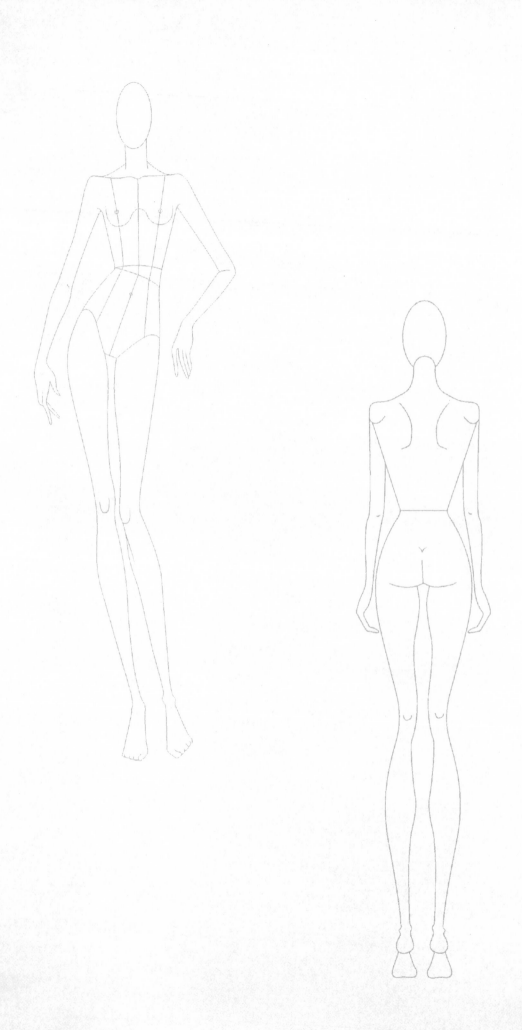

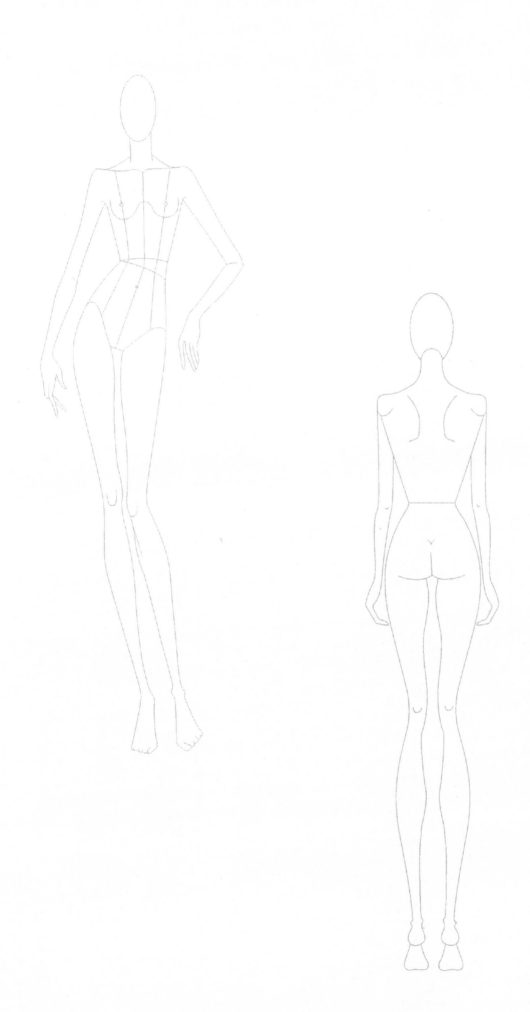

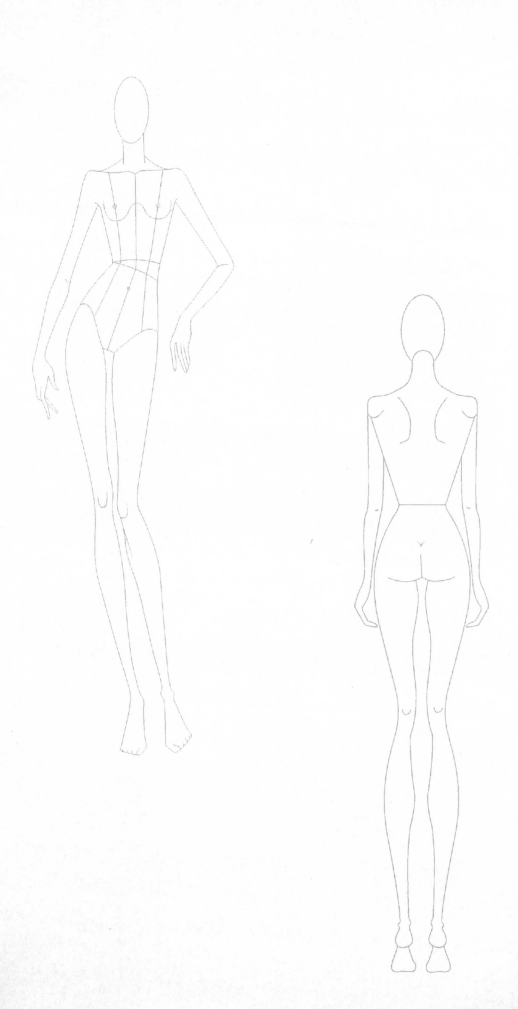

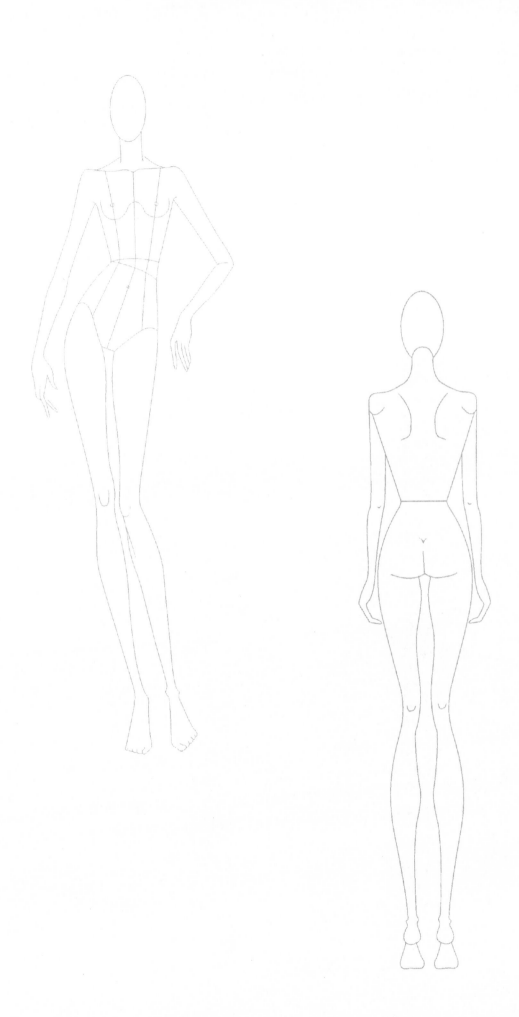

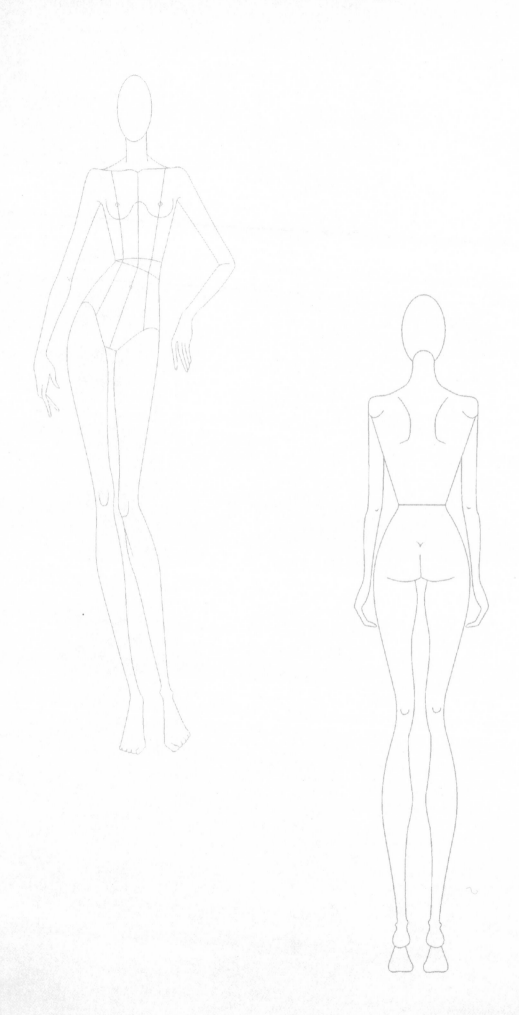

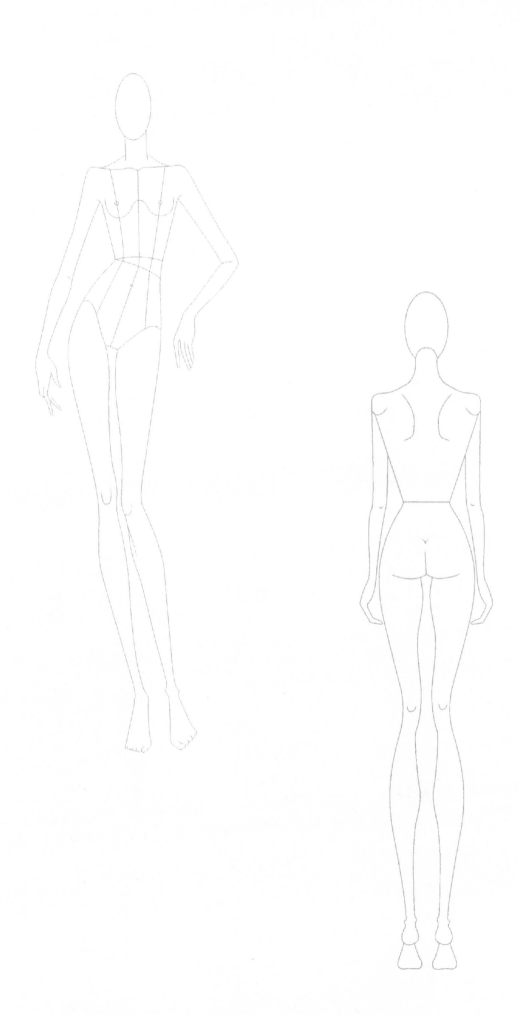

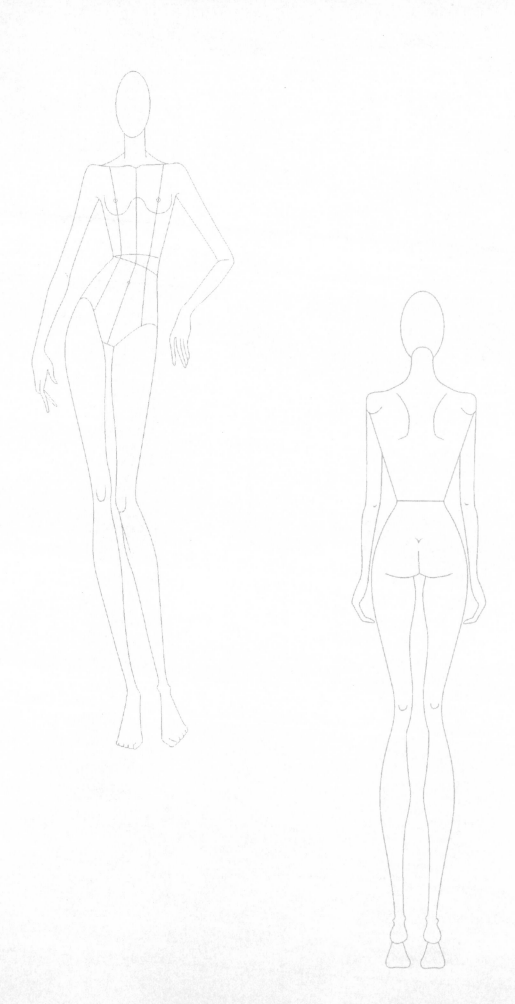

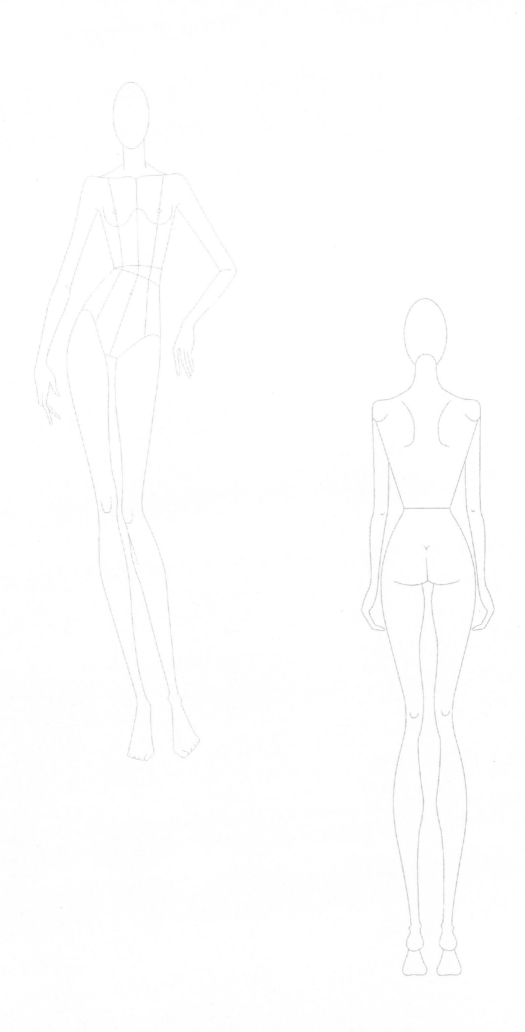

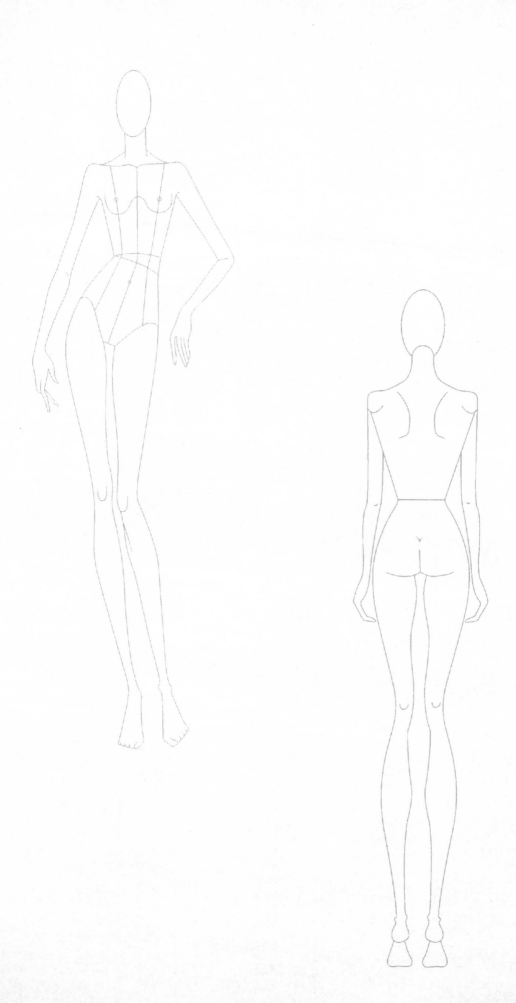

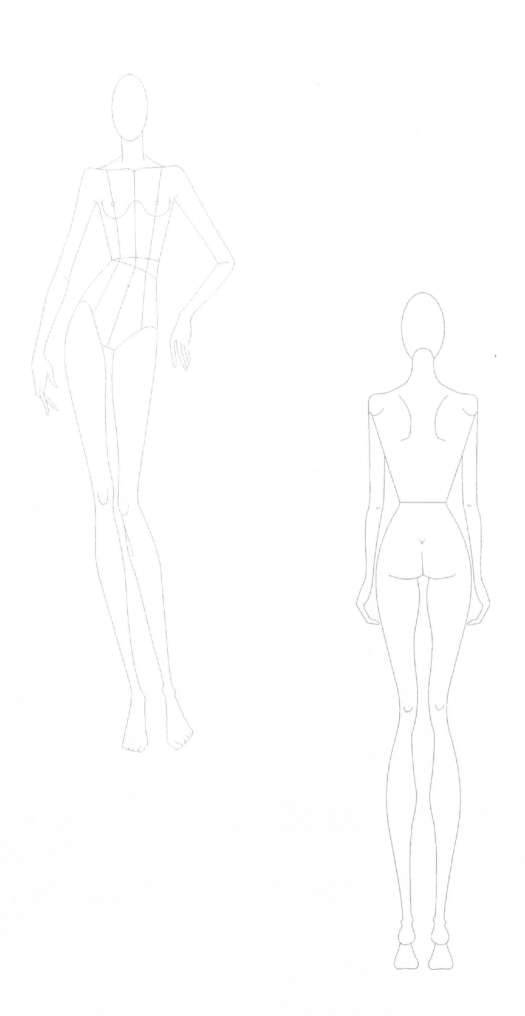

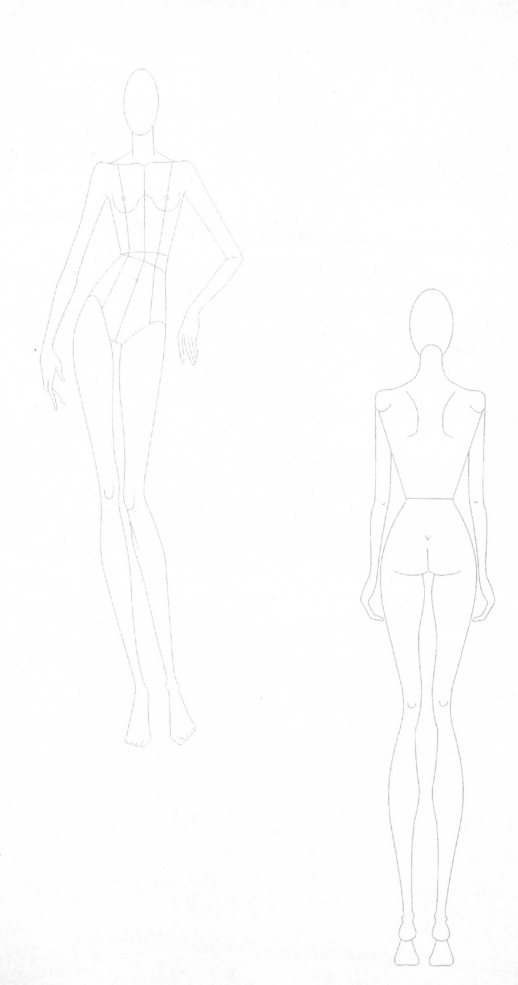

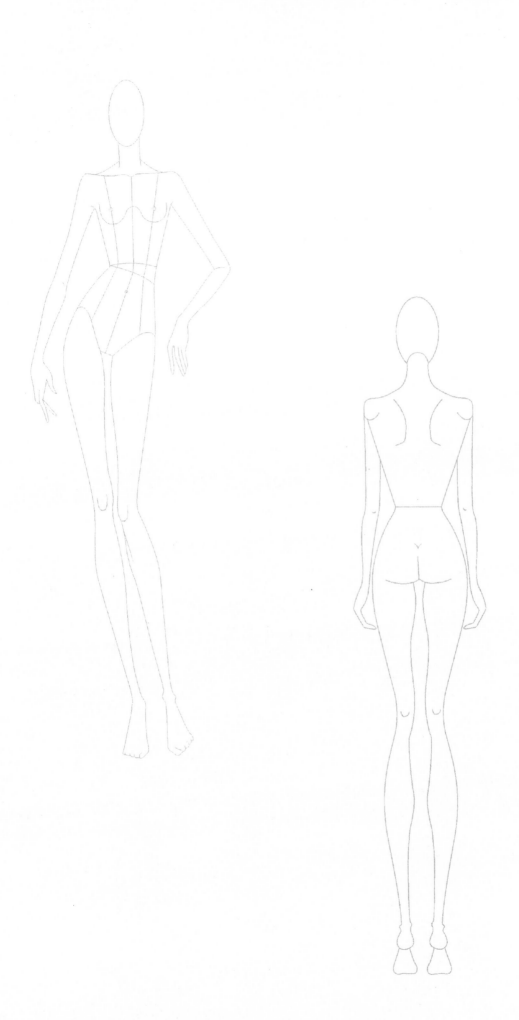

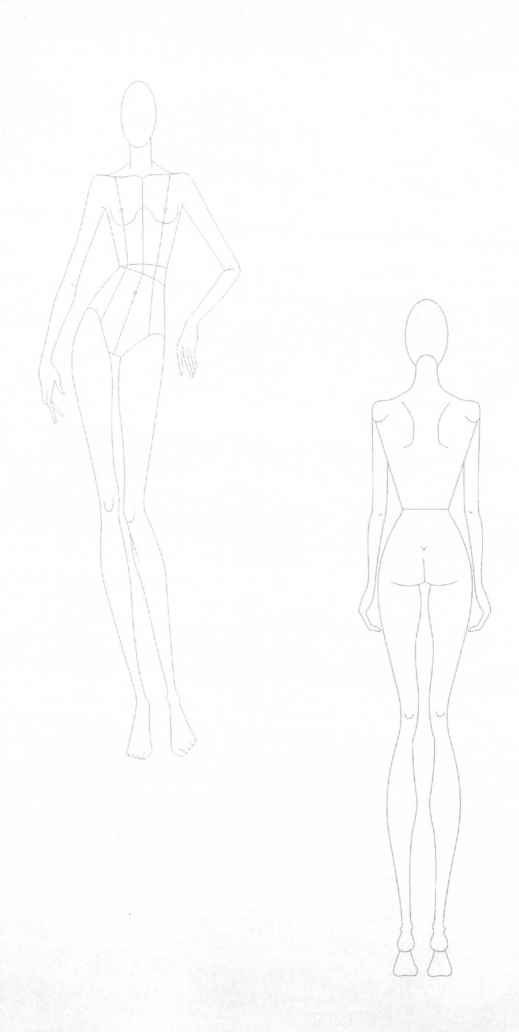